Technology and us

Wh … s of a person? Here are thre…

you … les and arms and legs, so that you can move about, get food and make things;

you have a *brain*, which you use to remember and imagine things, and work out what you need to do;

finally you have *senses*, like seeing and hearing, so that you can find out what is going on around you, and communicate with other people.

You can do quite a lot with your body, brain and senses.

Without any help at all, most of us can jump a stream a metre wide, remember a list of three or four things to buy when we go shopping, and shout a message to someone 50 metres away.

But for harder tasks we need help, and that's where technology comes in. With the help of a rope, we can swing across a wider river. With pencil and paper we can write a long shopping list and take it with us. With a mirror we can flash a message to someone many kilometres away. The rope, the pencil and paper and the mirror are all things that help us – simple technology helping us do more than we can do with body, brain and senses alone.

Today, there seems hardly any limit to what we can do with the help of technology. We can 'jump' across an ocean by aeroplane. We can 'remember' millions of words and pictures with a video recorder. And we can 'talk' to people the other side of the world by telephone.

There are three main parts to this LAUNCH PAD book: technology to help our *bodies*, to help our *brains*, and to help our *senses*.

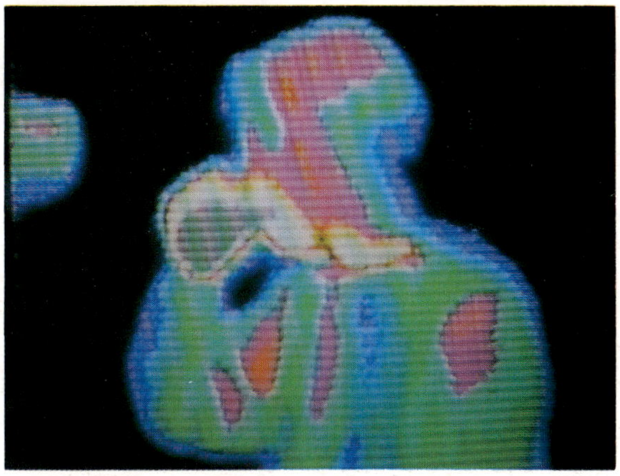

The HEAT CAMERA gives us an extra sense. It lets us 'see' whether things are hot or cold

Technology to help our bodies

Using energy

When you eat an apple, you take in some of the energy that was captured from the sun by the apple tree. You can use that energy to lift a weight, ride a bicycle or push a lawn-mower. Your body is a sort of engine which can do many things, but its power output is only a few hundred watts. Compare that to a small motor-mower, which has a power output of 2000 watts. That's like having four or five people to push the mower for you while you take a walk round the garden!

Today, people in Britain use much more energy every day than they can get from their own bodies – at least 100 times more. A great deal of energy is used to power our cars, heat our homes and run all our labour-saving machines. Factories use energy to make the things we use: as much energy goes into the making of one car as that car will use to go about 20 000 miles.

In Britain we depend on energy for nearly everything we do. On average each one of us uses about 30 times as much energy every day as a person in Ethiopia. Almost all our energy comes from coal, gas, oil or uranium. To make it useful we change it into different forms – like electricity, which is a convenient way of bringing energy from a power station into our homes.

This section of the book is about *energy technology* – the things in LAUNCH PAD that show how energy can be changed and stored and used.

If there were no power stations in Britain we would need 80 million people, all pedalling at top speed, to generate all the electricity we need on a cold winter evening. That's more than the whole population of the country!

ENERGY STORE

In the ENERGY STORE you convert *chemical* energy (from the food you have eaten) to *height* energy; this turns to *kinetic* energy (energy of motion) when the water runs back down again. The turbine converts this to *electrical* energy which the lamp and siren convert to *light* and *sound* energy.

But at every stage of conversion, some of the energy goes astray – mostly into *heat* energy.

Electricity can be produced from converting many different forms of energy.

Around one-quarter of the world's electricity is supplied by *hydro-electric power,* which uses the kinetic energy of flowing water to drive turbines directly.

Most power stations in Britain use coal or oil as a source of chemical energy; when they are burnt this is released as heat energy, and is used to turn water into high-pressure steam. Energy from the pressure of the expanding steam is used to drive turbines, which then generate electricity.

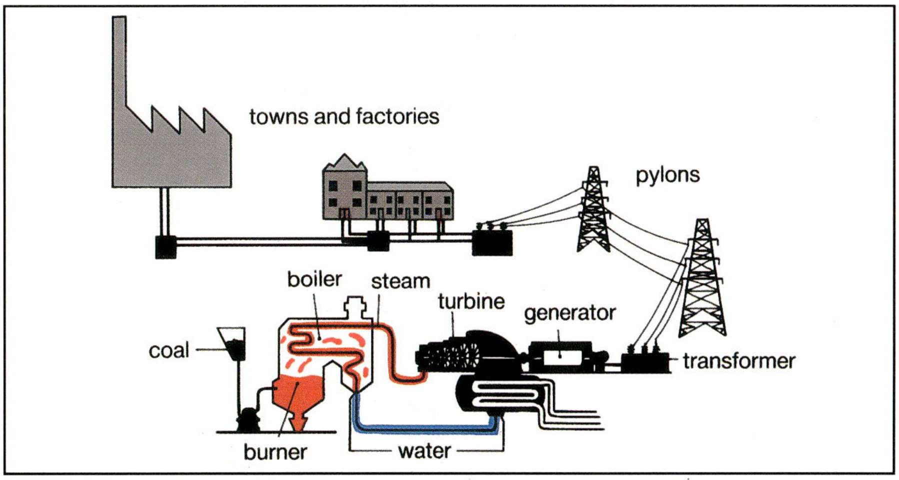

AIR VIEWS LTD

In Dinorwig in Wales, there is a power station which uses water to store the energy produced by other power stations as height energy. At night there is little demand for electricity, so spare electricity is used to pump water up to a reservoir at the top of a mountain.

When extra electricity is needed during the day, the water is allowed to flow back down and drive the turbines, just as it does in the ENERGY STORE exhibit. About three-quarters of the electricity used to pump the water up is regenerated in this way.

ELECTRIC MOTOR

The ELECTRIC MOTOR is one of the great labour-saving inventions: it has an enormous number of uses because it is clean, compact and makes efficient use of an easily available energy source.

MAN-VOLKSWAGEN

Electric bus in West Germany: the batteries are carried on a trailer behind the bus and are shown being charged.

Electric motors are used in many domestic tools and appliances – food-mixers, hair-driers, electric drills and so on.

Cars powered by electric motors would be cleaner and quieter than cars powered by petrol. But, so far, no battery of a reasonable size has been invented that can store as much energy as there is in a tank of petrol.

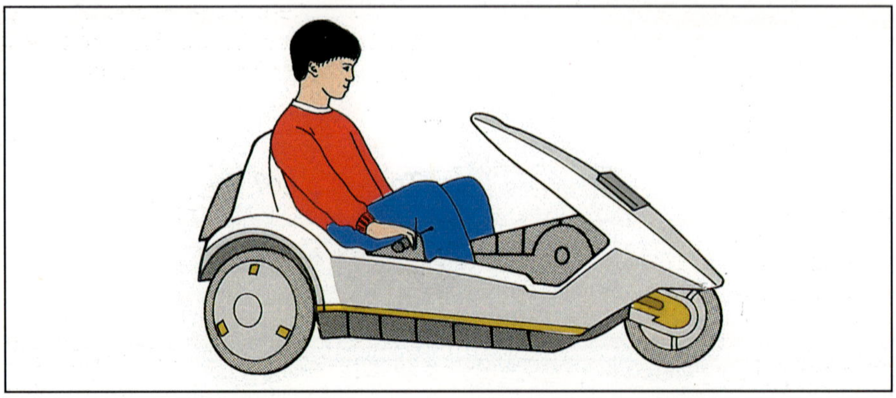

MUSEUM LINK – Electric gadgets

Look for gadgets with electric motors in the *Domestic Appliances* gallery.

The motor in this exhibit came from a C5 electric vehicle.

LAUNCH PAD at large – Motors at work

Look out for electric motors. How many of them have worked for you, and your family, today?

Tick them on the list and try to add some more:

Automatic door	Lift	_________________
Car (starter)	Model car or train	_________________
Cassette player	Vacuum cleaner	_________________
Electric train	Video	_________________
Escalator	Washing machine	_________________
Hair-drier	_________________	_________________

LAUNCH PAD at home – Measure your leg-power

Use this simple method to measure the power of your legs:

1 Weigh yourself, and work out your weight in kilograms. (1 stone is about 6.3 kilograms.)

2 Find a staircase, with 'normal height' steps.

3 Ask a friend to count out seconds from a watch or clock while you walk or run up the stairs.
How many stairs do you climb in two seconds?

4 Multiply your weight by the number of stairs you climbed in two seconds. The answer is, roughly, your leg-power in watts.

LAUNCH PAD Quiz – Paying for energy

In Britain a typical family's energy bills (gas, electricity, petrol, etc) add up in one year to

less than £350?
£350 to £700?
more than £700?

(Answer on page 49)

LAUNCH PAD Quiz – The sun's power

'The sun sends out as much energy in one second as we use on Earth in a hundred years.'

True or false?
(Answer on page 49)

ELECTRIC GENERATOR

The ELECTRIC GENERATOR has coils and magnets – just like the electric motor. You supply energy by turning the handle, and the generator changes some of this energy into electricity. This generator came from a motor-cycle.

In a power station the generators work in the same way, but they use electromagnets instead of permanent magnets and are powered by huge steam turbines.

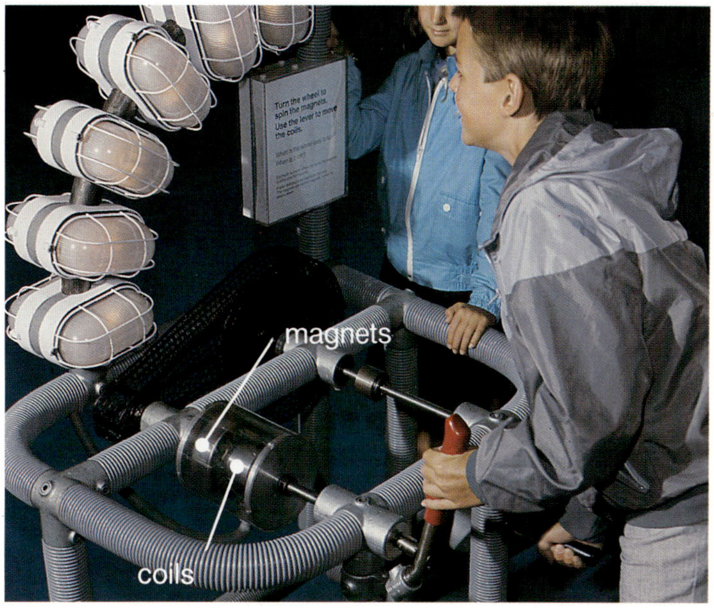

PLASMA BALL

When electricity flows through the gas in the PLASMA BALL, it creates *plasma,* made of atoms which have had some of their electrons knocked away. Energy from the electricity is changed into light – just as it is in a lightning flash.

In the exhibit a mixture of gases produces several different colours at once. Fluorescent lamps and neon signs also produce light from plasma.

TURNTABLE

All moving objects have movement energy, called *kinetic energy.*

The kinetic energy stored by something spinning depends on two things:

- its shape (or the way its weight is distributed), and
- how fast it spins.

On the TURNTABLE people spin faster when they pull themselves towards the centre than when they lean out.

When you lean out, your body traces out a larger circle than when you lean in, so it moves faster for the same rate of turning.

When you lean in, you go a smaller distance each turn. Your rate of turning must increase to give the same speed – so you spin faster.

Of course, some parts of your body trace a small circle even when you lean out – your hands and feet, for example. What matters is where your weight is concentrated.

Skaters use this idea to make themselves spin faster. When they pull their arms in, more of their weight is concentrated near the centre so they spin faster.

MUSEUM LINK – Flywheels

Find the flywheels on some of the large steam engines on the ground floor of the Museum.

Where else in the Museum can you find flywheels?

Stars obey this rule too.

This star is at the centre of the Crab nebula. Since the star was first observed in the year 1054, it has imploded to become about 10^{-8} of its original diameter. Since its weight is now so concentrated near the centre, its speed of rotation has increased enormously – from perhaps one turn per month to its present observed rate of 30 turns per second.

Flywheels make use of this idea too, though in the opposite way. They are designed to store as much energy as possible when they spin. Most of their weight is usually concentrated near the rim, away from the centre.

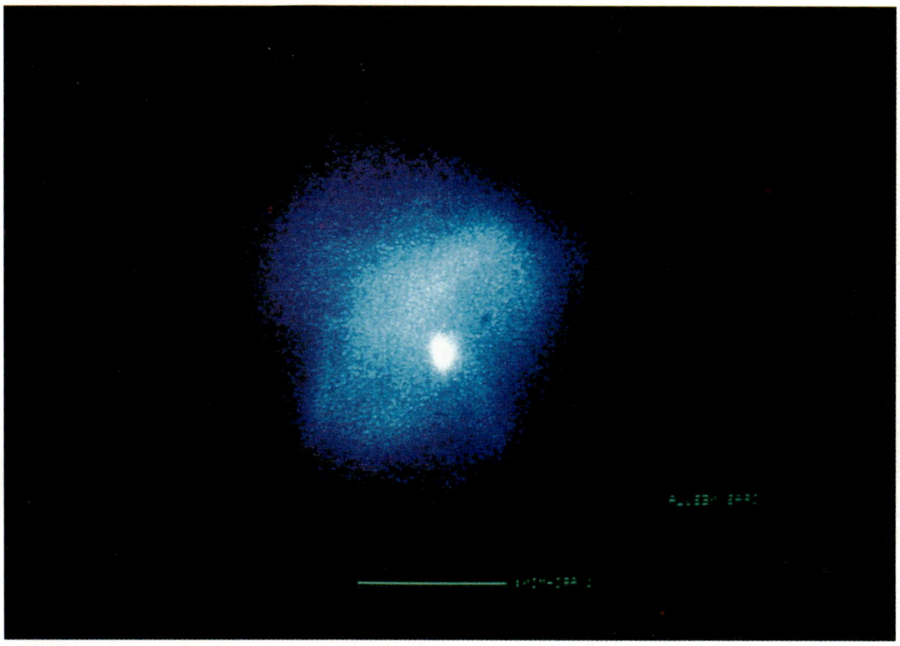

HARVARD-SMITHSONIAN CENTRE FOR ASTROPHYSICS

This flywheel is 5.5 metres in diameter and weighs 22 tonnes. Its large size and great weight help it to store a lot of energy.

GEAR WHEELS

GEAR WHEELS are used to change the speed of things that turn, in cars and in many other machines.

LAUNCH PAD Quiz – Gear wheels

Gear wheels were invented

about 100 years ago?
about 500 years ago?
about 2000 years ago?

(Answer on page 49)

PULLEYS AND BELTS

PULLEYS AND BELTS can do the same job, and also carry energy from one part of a machine to another. Bicycles use a chain instead of a belt. The chain joins two gear wheels of different sizes.

LAUNCH PAD at home – Check your cycle gearing

Take your bicycle outside and *carefully* turn it upside down.

How many times does the back wheel go round when the pedals go round once? This is the 'speed ratio'.

If your cycle has a gear change, see what difference it makes when you change gear.

If your cycle doesn't have a gear change, count the number of teeth on each of the two main gear-wheels. Can you see any connection between these numbers and the speed ratio?

HUMAN BATTERY

Batteries convert chemical energy into electrical energy. Most batteries are made of two different plates, often metals, and an electrolyte – something which conducts electricity and is decomposed by it. In the HUMAN BATTERY exhibit, your slightly damp and salty hands are the electrolyte. Your body conducts and so joins the plates.

AIR POWER

AIR POWER is a motor driven by the pressure of air from a blower. The air has to be let into the cylinder in bursts, at just the right moments, to push the piston and make the motor run smoothly. A car engine also has cylinders and pistons. It uses hot gas, made by burning petrol, instead of compressed air.

LAUNCH PAD Quiz – Pulleys

When wheel A goes round once, how many times does wheel B go round?

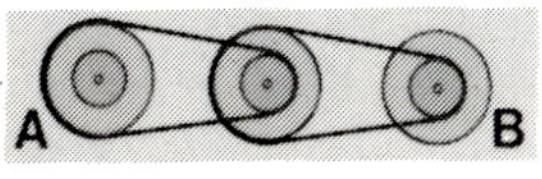

(Answer on page 49)

Moving around

To win an Olympic medal for sprinting you have to run faster than 20 mph (36 kilometres per hour). To win the London marathon you have to cover the first 20 miles (32 kilometres) in well under two hours.

Today we can all break these records. We do it when we go on a journey – like travelling to London to visit LAUNCH PAD. To help us we use cars, buses, trains and many other forms of transport. We can even go to America and back in a day by flying on Concorde, or to the Moon and back in a week in an Apollo space-craft.

As well as going on journeys ourselves, we need to transport materials from place to place. Water is a good example. Every day each person in Britain uses 120 litres (27 gallons) of clean water, often piped from a reservoir many kilometres away. Think what it would be like if you had to fetch your own water, instead of just turning on the tap. 120 litres of water weighs as much as six heavy suitcases!

Many everyday things have to be transported from even further away, like bananas from the West Indies, videos from Japan, and meat from New Zealand.

This section of the book is about *transport technology* – the exhibits in LAUNCH PAD that help you find the answers to questions like these: what makes a plane fly? How is grain moved on farms and in factories? What keeps a train on the rails? And why do some cars use more petrol than others?

To help design new aeroplanes, engineers often build models and test them in a wind tunnel. You can do the same at the FLIGHT TEST exhibit.

AIR JET

In the AIR JET exhibit, the air pushes against the underside of the ball, and this keeps it up.

But why does it stay in the middle of the air jet?

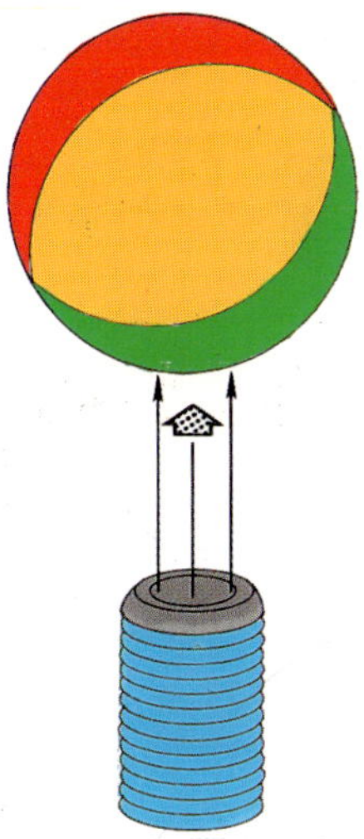

When a ball is hanging in air which is not moving, this air pushes on the ball equally from all directions. But when the air around the ball starts moving in one direction, things change.

The faster the air moves past a surface, the smaller is the push or air pressure on that surface.

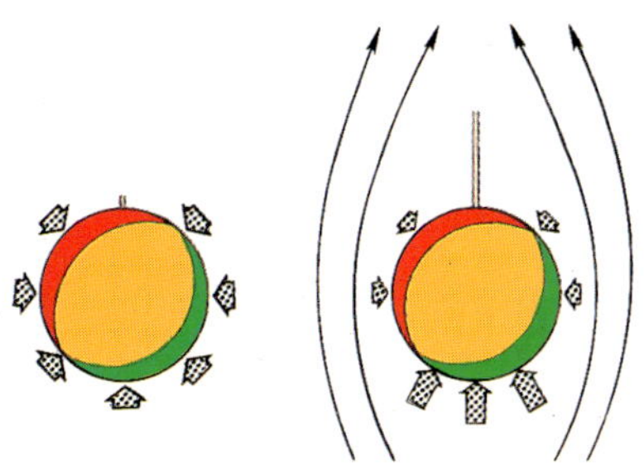

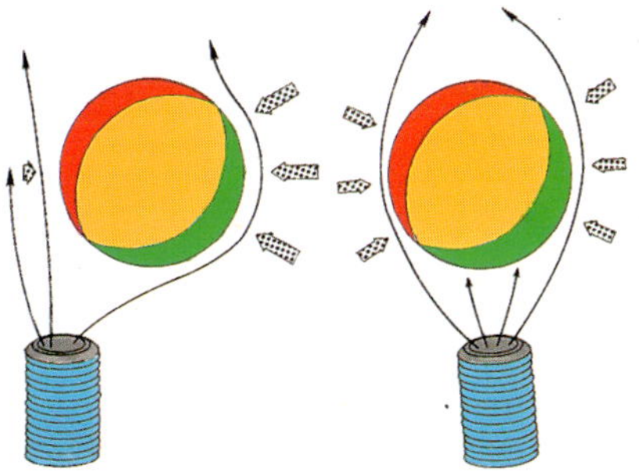

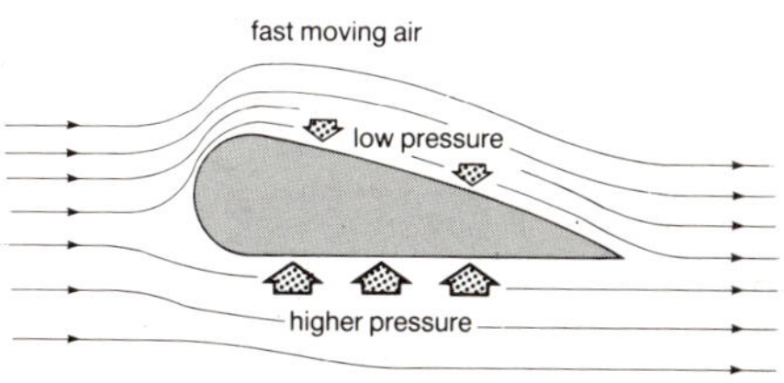

The air moves fastest in the middle of the jet so that is where pressure on the ball is smallest. If you move the air jet away from the ball, then the pressure on the side nearest the centre of the air stream is smaller than the pressure on the side furthest from the centre. So the ball is pushed back into the air jet until the pressure on both sides is the same.

You can see the same effect if you balance a ping-pong ball in a garden hose. And this effect also keeps birds and aeroplanes in the air.

The wing of a bird or an aeroplane is shaped so that, as it flies, the air moves faster over the top than past the bottom.

The upward pressure on the bottom of the wing is greater than the downward pressure on the top of the wing. And this pressure difference keeps birds and aeroplanes up.

LAUNCH PAD at home –

Vacuum cleaner air jet

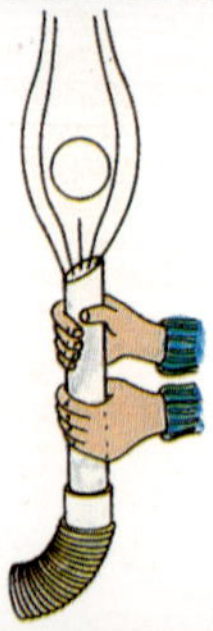

This experiment needs a vacuum cleaner that can blow as well as suck.

Ask to borrow the vacuum cleaner, and use it to make your own air jet exhibit with a table-tennis ball.

CAR DRAG TEST

When a new car is designed it has to be tested for 'wind drag' – the force of the wind which tries to slow it down when it is going at high speed. If the shape of the car is right it will have a low wind drag, which means it will use less petrol.

At the CAR DRAG TEST exhibit you can compare model cars of different shapes.

SLOW BUBBLES

These air bubbles move very slowly up a long tube. This is because the liquid in the SLOW BUBBLES exhibit is very thick and sticky, and stops them going any faster.

The same rules apply to parachutes. They come down slowly because the 'thickness' of the air stops them going any faster.

MUSEUM LINK – Car shapes

In the *Road Transport* gallery, look at the way the shape of cars has changed over 100 years.

LAUNCH PAD at large –

Shapes of cars and lorries

Look at the shapes of cars and lorries. Which parts show that the designer has tried to reduce the wind drag?

Look out for a car with a 'spoiler' at the back. It helps to control the way the air flows past the car.

How many lorries have a spoiler on the roof of the driver's cab?

WATER PUMP

The WATER PUMP exhibit is a suction pump worked by hand. It uses the pressure of the atmosphere to push water up into the barrel. The valves ensure that water flows through the pump in only one direction.

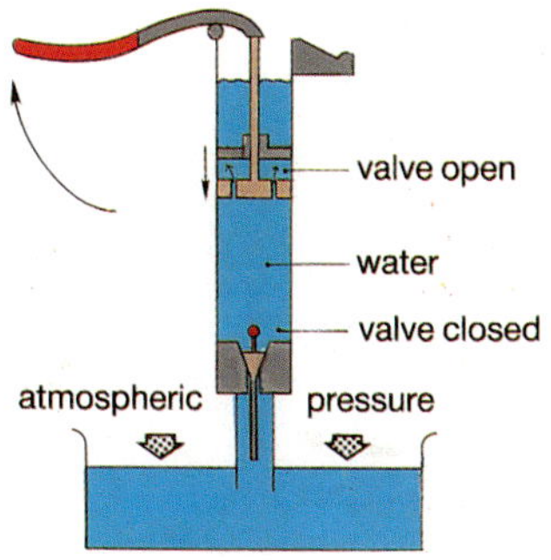

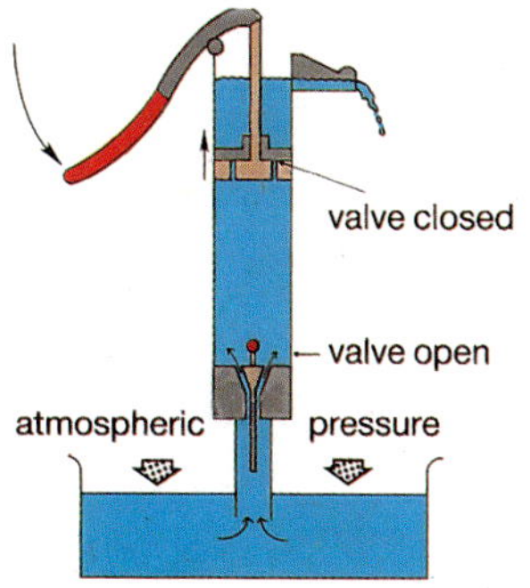

Atmospheric pressure can raise water over fairly small heights. But, if the pump is deeper than about 30 feet (9 metres), the weight of the column of water that it is trying to lift is too great to be balanced by the upward force of atmospheric pressure, and the pump does not work.

Hand-operated suction pumps are easy to build and repair, and are much used in India and Africa.

MARK EDWARDS/EARTHSCAN

The first pumping systems that supplied water to whole towns were built around 1500. One was built in 1582 at London Bridge. It pumped water from the Thames through a network of pipes to individual houses, and helped improve health and hygiene in London.

The pumping machine was very large, but the machinery used was quite simple. Waterwheels drove forcer pumps which used long plungers to force water up.

Most water-supply systems are now centrally organised. Water is pumped from rivers and stored in large reservoirs. It is cleaned and then pumped into small local reservoirs on high ground, or to water towers. It then flows under gravity through a network of pipes to where it is needed.

Every day in Britain, each person uses about 120 litres of water. The Thames supplies over one billion litres each day.

THAMES WATER AUTHORITY

DIVERS

Submarines – and fish – have 'buoyancy tanks' to help them float or sink. The buoyancy tank inside these DIVERS is a pocket of air. When you squeeze the plastic tube, you squeeze the water in the main tank too. This squeezes the air pocket in the diver, until it is so small that it cannot keep him afloat.

LAUNCH PAD at home – Drinking-straw diver

Make your own diver in a large plastic drinks bottle.

1 Use a drinking straw for the diver. Cut the straw in half and block up one end with a small piece of Plasticine or Blu-tack.

2 Stick a larger piece of Plasticine or Blu-tack round the other end, to weight it – but don't block this end. Add extra bits until the 'diver' almost sinks when you put him into a glass of water – but not quite.

3 Fill the lemonade bottle with water, put the diver in, and put the lid on the bottle tightly.

4 Squeeze the bottle to make the diver sink.

Can you explain how it works?

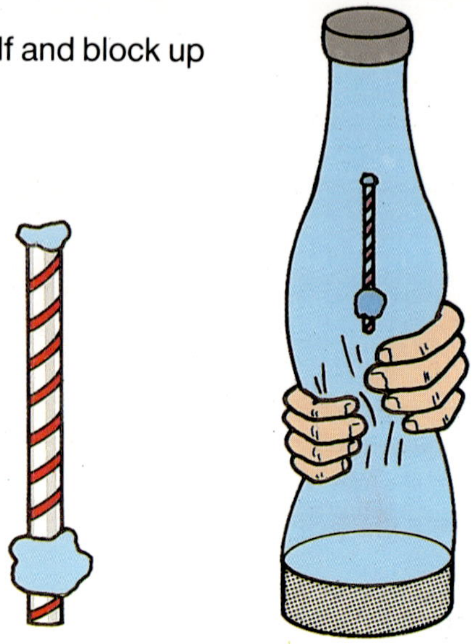

GRAIN PIT

Many different machines are used in factories and on farms to move grain and other solid materials. Some of them are in the GRAIN PIT exhibit.

The spiral 'corkscrew' which lifts the grain up inside a tube is said to have been invented by Archimedes more than 2200 years ago.

TRAIN WHEELS

Trains run on 'coned' wheels – with a sloping edge – like the ones in this picture. The TRAIN WHEELS exhibit shows that this shape helps them stay on the track. They even steer themselves round the curves.

MUSEUM LINK – Train wheels

Look at some of the locomotives in the *Rail Transport* gallery. Do they all have coned wheels?

LAUNCH PAD Quiz – Space shuttle

How many people, pulling in a tug-of-war, would produce as much force as the engines of the space shuttle do when it takes off?

about 200?
about 2000?
about 20 000?
(Answer on page 49)

LAUNCH PAD Quiz – Speed record

'In 1900 no one had ever travelled at 100 mph (160 kilometres per hour).'

True or false? (Answer on page 49)

MAGNETIC RIVER

Under the glass on the MAGNETIC RIVER exhibit there is part of an electric motor. The usual type of motor makes things spin round. But this is a *linear motor* – it makes pieces of metal move along in a straight line.

The linear motor makes a moving pattern of magnetism which flows along above the glass. Instead of using ordinary magnets moving along on a conveyor belt, the linear motor uses a large number of electromagnets, or coils.

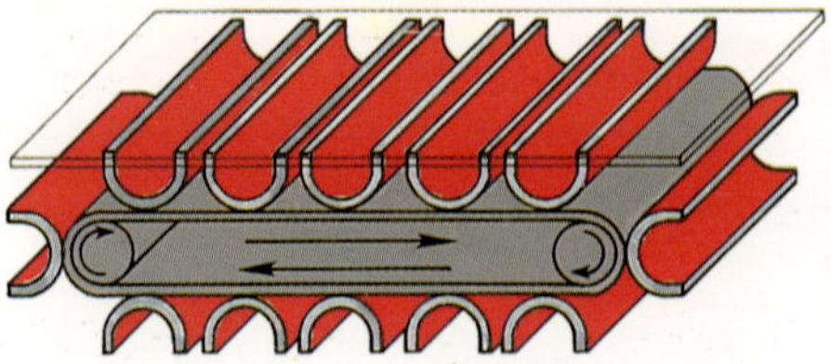

Changing electric currents flow through the coils in turn, and create a moving magnetic field above the glass.

A piece of metal, such as aluminium, is dragged along by this 'magnetic river'. This happens because the changing magnetism produced by the coils makes electric currents flow inside the metal plate. (This process is known as *induction*.) These currents make the plate behave like a magnet too, and it is pulled along by the magnetism from the coils.

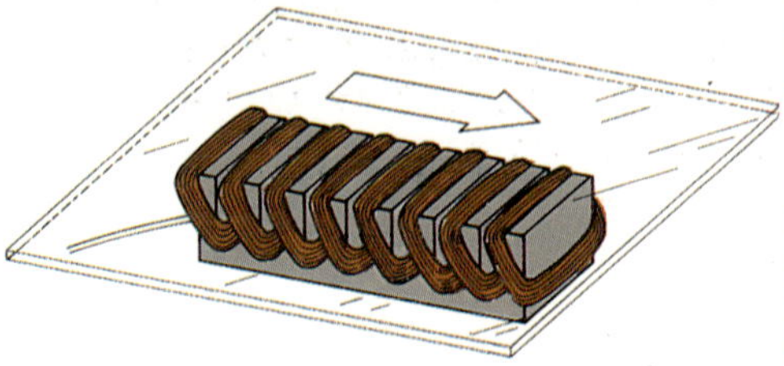

The plate and the part with the coils are together known as a *linear induction motor.*

The special rail cars that run between Birmingham International Station and Birmingham Airport are powered by linear induction motors. The coils are under the floor of the rail car, and the long metal plate runs along the track, as you can see in the foreground of the photograph.

GEC TRANSPORTATION PROJECTS LTD

MAGNETIC PULL

The MAGNETIC PULL exhibit shows another way you can use magnetism to move things. A coil of wire has been wound round the tube. When a strong electric current is put through this wire, the coil is made into an electromagnet, and the metal rod is pulled into the tube – provided the rod is made from a magnetic material.

BEARING KIT

Rolling bearings are used in many machines where one part has to move past another – such as where the wheels of a bicycle are fixed to the frame. Bearings reduce friction, which wears things away and wastes energy.

You can see the balls which reduce friction in this giant-sized BEARING KIT.

LAUNCH PAD at home – Marble ball-bearing

Make your own ball-bearing using marbles.

1 Find a round margarine or yogurt carton. Cut the bottom off with scissors to make a tray with low sides.

2 Put marbles round the edge of the tray.

3 Make a lid from another plastic carton – a bit larger than the first one. Now your ball-bearing is ready for use.

4 Lay a heavy book on the ball-bearing so that it balances. Will it spin round easily?

Can you think of some ways to make the marble ball-bearing work better?

Making and building

Have you ever tried to count the number of bones in one of your hands? There are 27 altogether. They are loosely held together so that they can move, and there are dozens of muscles to control them.

Because we can control them so well, our hands are very useful to us. We can use them for *making things,* for example. To do this we often need to use special tools as well – like pliers, scissors or a saw – so that we can tackle jobs which our hands cannot do by themselves.

To make bigger things – buildings and bridges – we need larger tools, like cranes. Centuries ago people managed to build enormous cathedrals without the help of modern tools, but they took a very long time to do so: just the front of St Alban's cathedral took 40 years to build.

A CRANE is like a long, strong arm – useful to help with building bridges and other large structures.

Today we know more about the materials we use and the stresses and strains in them when they are made into buildings. This means we can build taller buildings which use less material – but they may not last as long, nor look as beautiful, as the great buildings of 700 or 800 years ago.

New materials have been invented too, such as plastics. They are extremely useful – and not just as substitutes for older materials. If you look round your home you will find plastics being used to do many jobs which no other material could do as well.

This section of the book is about *technology for making and building things* – exhibits in LAUNCH PAD that show how materials are used and tested, and how to build structures that won't fall down.

LAUNCH PAD at large – Arches

Look out for buildings with arches. There may even be an arch on your home, and you can see several arches – and some domes – on buildings near the Science Museum.

Notice the shape of the bricks or stones, and the shapes of the arches. Are they always semi-circles?

ARCH BRIDGE

Early bridge builders may have been inspired by natural arches carved by the wind and waves. Amongst the first bridges they built was the ARCH BRIDGE.

Bridge builders (civil engineers) start by building a strong shape of wood or metal, called a *centring*. The stone or concrete arch is then built on top of the centring. When the *key stone* is in place, the centring is taken away.

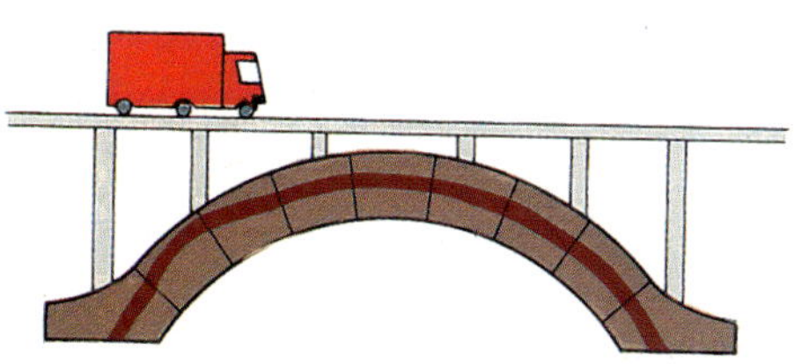

The weight of the key stone is a force pushing down. It is held up by two forces pushing upwards from either side. These pushing forces are passed from section to section through the arch bridge, and so to the ground.

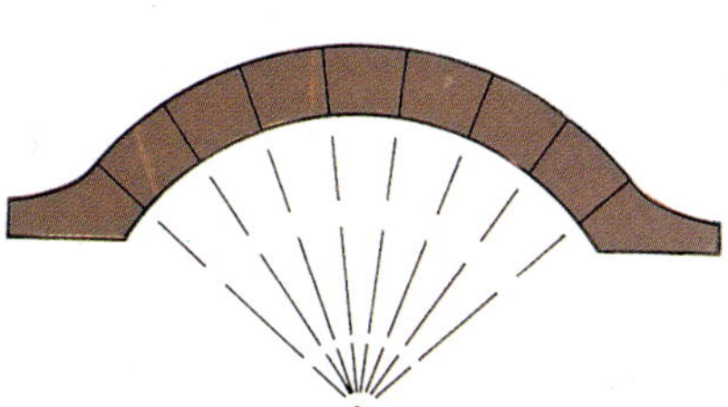

The arch has to be carefully designed: the lines of the forces that balance the weight of the bridge, and its load, must stay inside the material of the arch itself.

BRITISH GEOLOGICAL SURVEY

The LAUNCH PAD arch is part of a circle, just like Roman arches. But engineers can now make low bridges with very wide spans, so modern arch bridges are of many different shapes.

STRESS PATTERNS

We cannot see the waves in a ray of light, yet it contains millions of very short waves. Normally light waves vibrate in many different directions, but they can be *polarised* so that they vibrate in one direction only. This happens when light goes through a sheet of polarising material.

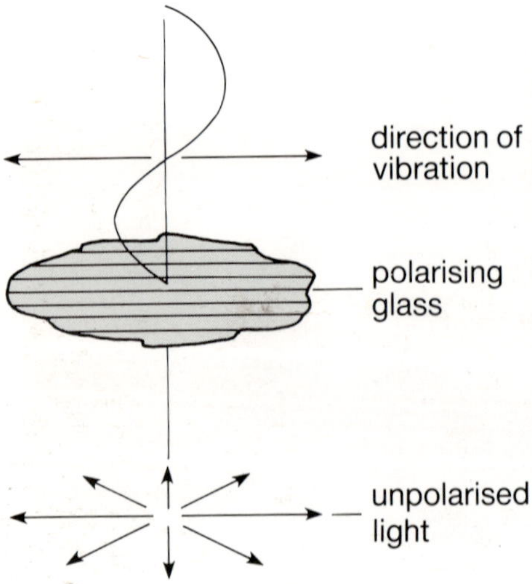

The polarised light waves are vibrating in one direction only. All the rest of the light has been absorbed.

Polaroid sunglasses are also made from polarising material. So if the polarising direction of the sunglasses and polarising material is parallel, most light gets through. If they are at right angles, no light gets through at all.

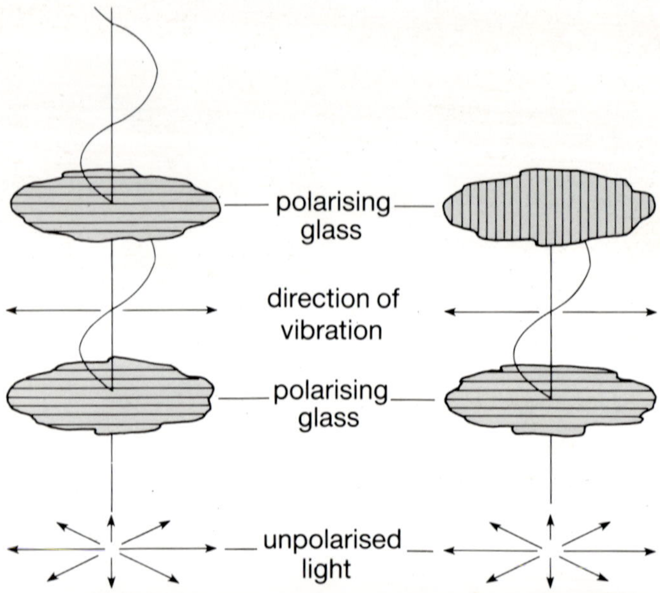

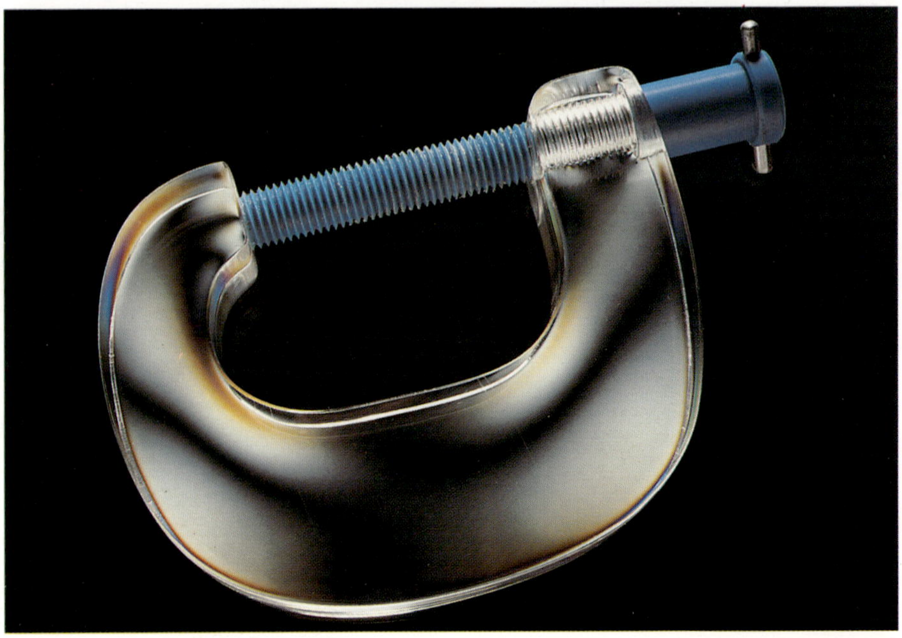

In the STRESS PATTERNS exhibit, you can put a plastic spanner – *stressed* – on the light box and look at it through polaroid glasses. It looks coloured, so some light must be getting through.

This is because stressing the plastic spanner shifts some of the atoms in the plastic, so that the light is split into *two* beams, polarised in different directions. So some light is able to get through the polaroid glasses, no matter what their direction.

But the two beams travel through the plastic at different speeds, so one gets ahead of the other. When they meet again at the glasses, they are out of step with one another. So, instead of just re-combining, they *interfere*.

This causes the colours you see, because the stressed plastic acts like a prism to split up the white light from the light box into coloured light. Each different amount of stress in the plastic causes interference which cuts out more of one colour than of the others.

This effect is called *photo-elasticity*.

Engineers use photoelasticity to predict stresses in buildings or machines before they are built. They first make a scale model of the structure in plastic. The model is then stressed, as the real structure would be, and is examined between polarisers. Very high stresses show up as closely packed bands, and the amount of stress at any point can be calculated quite accurately. Engineers can then predict whether the real structure will be able to withstand the stresses it will be subjected to.

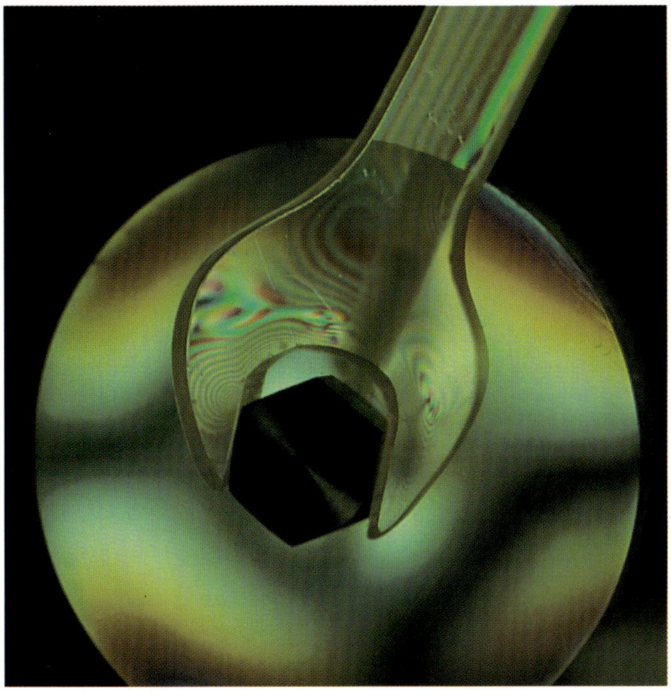

SHARPLES STRESS ENGINEERING LTD

Rather like a contour map, the closer together the coloured bands are, the more sharply the stress is changing there.

This photoelastic image shows the high stress points in a model of a Toblerone bar – and shows that it is likely to break between the pieces, just as intended.

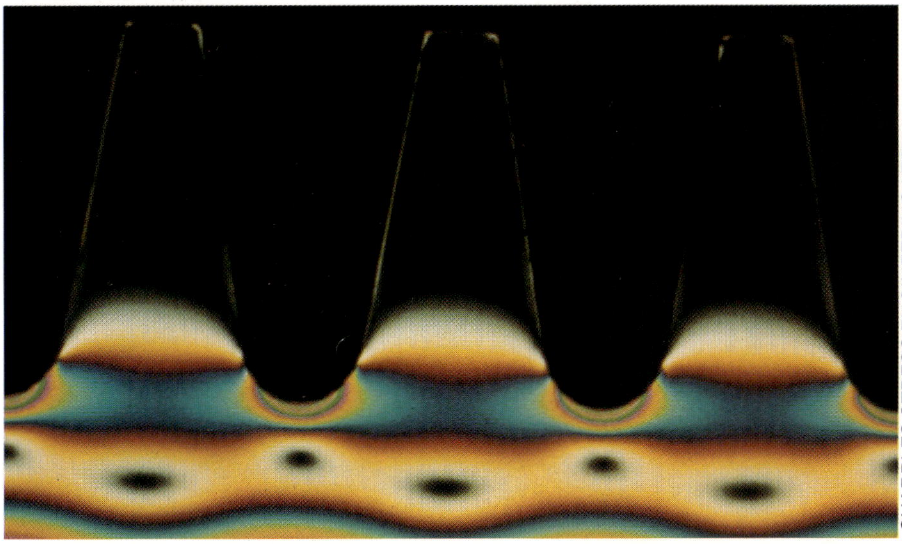

SHARPLES STRESS ENGINEERING LTD

LAUNCH PAD Quiz – Before plastics

50 years ago, before plastics were common, what material do you think was used to make each of these:

carrier bags?
washing-up bowls?
babies' bottles?
(Answers on page 49)

METAL FATIGUE

If the piece of metal in the centre of the METAL FATIGUE exhibit is bent – or 'stressed' – a few times, it does not break. But after being bent a large number of times it begins to get 'tired' and breaks quite easily.

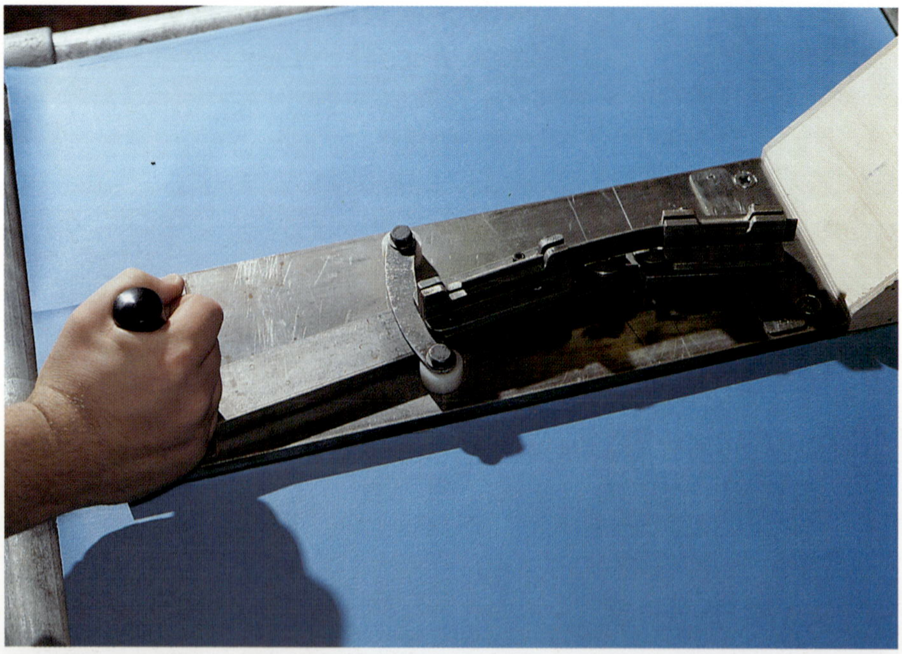

LAUNCH PAD at home – Stress patterns

Some plastic – like a transparent cassette box – shows the stress patterns left inside it when it was made:

1 Borrow a pair of *polaroid* sunglasses and put them on.

2 Hold a cassette box the way it is shown in the picture, so that it reflects the light from the sky (not the sun), or from an electric light, into your eyes.

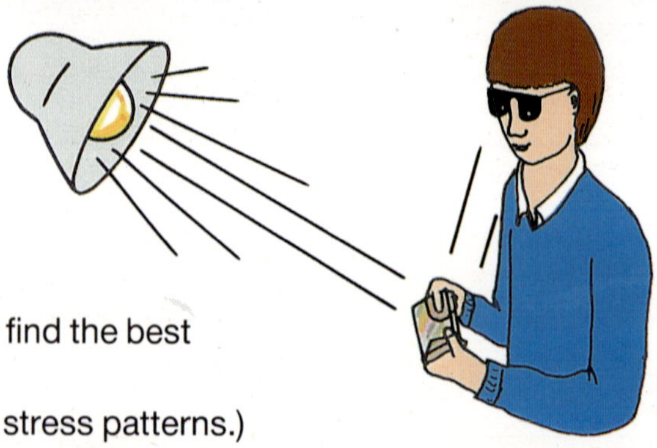

Can you see a coloured stress pattern? Tilt the box to find the best position.

Try some other pieces of plastic. (They won't all show stress patterns.)

LASER CUTTING demonstration

A powerful laser can make a beam which is like a needle of concentrated energy. Where this beam hits something it can produce so much heat that the material is vapourised. In this demonstration, the laser beam is cutting a piece of cloth. Stronger beams can cut plastic and even metal plates.

STRING STRUCTURE

In the STRING STRUCTURE exhibit a surprisingly strong 'table' can be made out of strings and struts. They clip together at the ends, but there are no rigid joints. The same method is used for cranes, tents and some bridges. With our bones and tendons we are all 'string structures' ourselves.

LAUNCH PAD Quiz – String structure

Here is a simple structure, made from five struts and five strings. It holds up a weight W.

Can you find one strut and one string which you could take away without the structure collapsing?

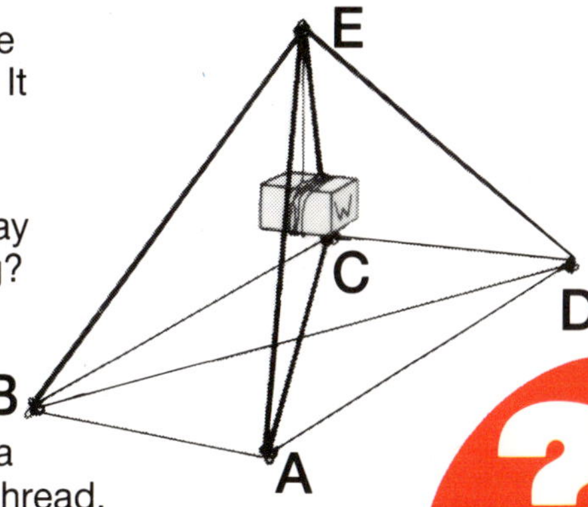

(Answer on page 49 – or make a model from pipe-cleaners and thread, and try it!)

ELECTRIC DUST

When you rub the plastic top of the ELECTRIC DUST box, you produce static electricity. This makes the small pieces of 'dust' jump up and down inside.

With many modern materials, static electricity can be a nuisance. It can also be useful – for cleaning dirty smoke, making photocopies, and painting round corners!

MUSEUM LINK – Bridges

Look at some bridge models in the *Roads, Bridges and Tunnels* gallery. Which ones are like arches? Which are more like 'string structures'?

MUSEUM LINK – Static electricity

You can watch a short video about the dangers of static electricity, in the *Electricity and Magnetism* gallery on the third floor.

SALT BOWL

When the air blower is off, the salt feels quite dry and solid. When it is on, the air blows the salt grains apart so that they can flow past each other, just like the molecules in a saucepan of water.

For this reason the SALT BOWL is called a *fluidised bed*.

If the air blows too fast, the grains will blow away. If it blows too slowly, the grains will not move at all. In a fluidised bed, the air blows at just the right rate to make the grains move past each other.

Fluidised beds are used to mix gases and solids very thoroughly together, so that chemical reactions between them take place quickly and efficiently.

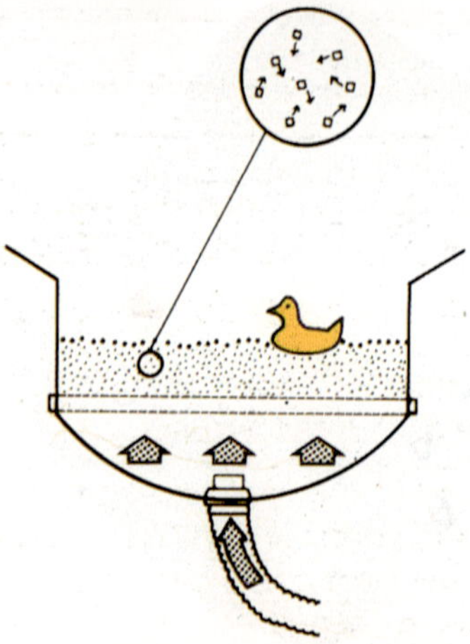

Coal burns more quickly in a fluidised bed and can provide much more heat than it would if burnt in a furnace of the same size. The coal particles are supported in a fluidised bed made by blowing air through sand.

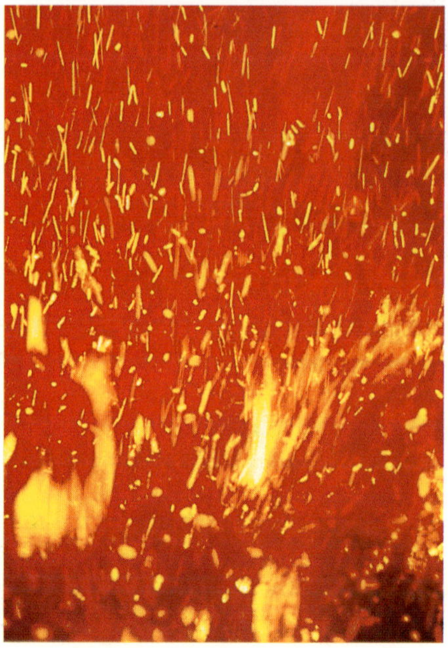

NCB

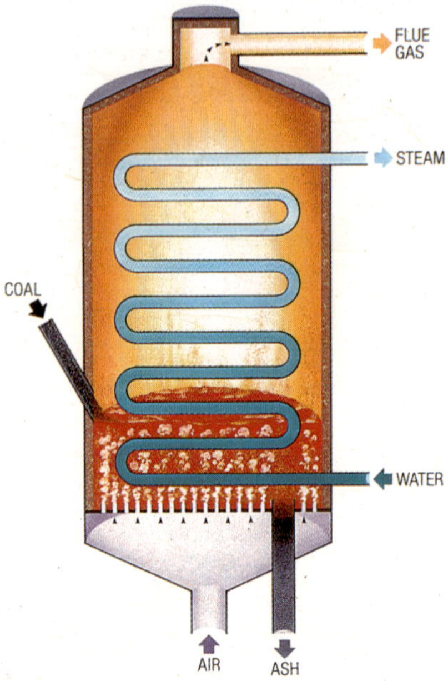

Peas and other vegetables are often frozen in a fluidised bed made by supporting them on a stream of very cold (−38 °C) fast-moving air.

FRIGO SCANDIA

BUBBLE SHEET

Detergents, such as washing-up liquid, are usually man-made materials. A small amount of detergent added to water makes it able to dissolve and remove grease, so that it cleans things better.

In the BUBBLE SHEET exhibit you can experiment with a large flat 'bubble' made mainly of water with a little detergent in it.

LAUNCH PAD at home – Electric paper

Try this simple experiment using static electricity:

1 Cut out some tiny spiky pieces from a tissue – like these:

2 Borrow the lid of an airtight polythene food container. Rub it on your clothes to charge it up, and then hold it above the pieces of tissue.

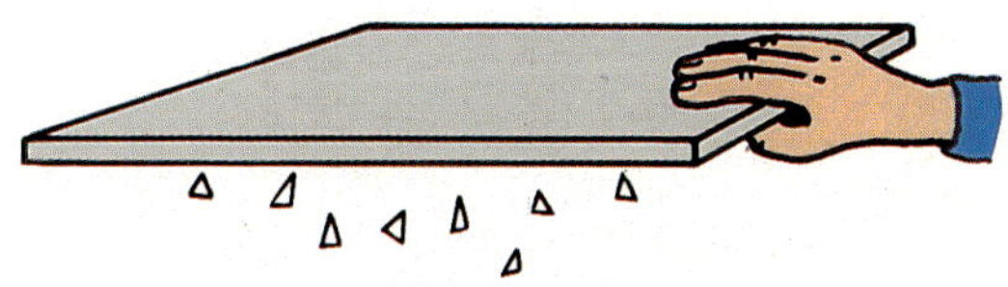

How high can you make the paper jump?

Try some other plastic things. Which ones charge up best?

LAUNCH PAD at home – Bubble sheet

You can make your own bubble sheet like this:

1 Bend a wire coat-hanger to make a square frame.

2 Wind some string along one of the sides nearest to the handle. This will help to soak up the bubble mixture.

3 Fill a large washing-up bowl with cold water, and stir in four tablespoons of washing-up liquid.

4 Put the frame into the bubble mixture so that it is completely covered. Then slowly slide it out, with the side with string on it at the top.

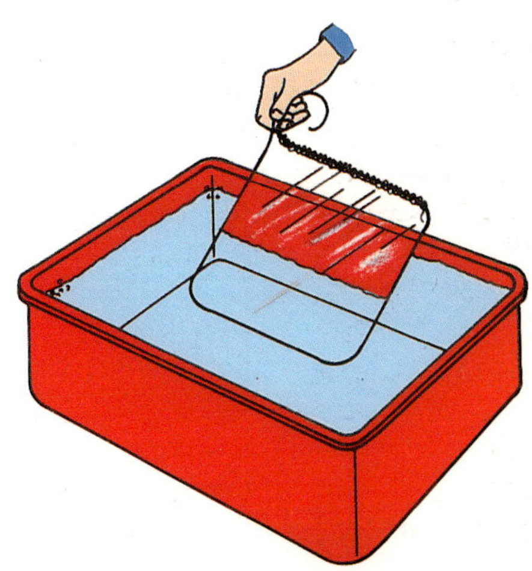

Can you see the bubble sheet stretched across the frame? What happens when you blow on it gently?

Can you hold your bubble sheet like a mirror, reflecting a bright surface, so that you can watch the colours?

(You can make a bubble sheet that lasts longer by adding up to eight tablespoonfuls of *glycerine* to the mixture. Glycerine is used in cooking and as a medicine. It can be bought at chemists', and is not poisonous.)

Technology to help our brains

Using information

There are 30 000 million tiny cells in your brain – called 'neurons'. Many of them are hard at work right now. Some are letting you see and read these words, by processing the images in your eyes. Others are used for thinking; they make it possible for you to understand what the words say.

Your brain is a powerful machine for storing and processing information. Many millions of neurons store your memories – all you can remember about everything that has ever happened to you, and much more that you are not even aware of knowing. Your brain controls the beating of your heart, too, and the way your food is digested.

But even with such powerful brains we still sometimes need help. We find it hard to remember all the phone numbers of our friends, for example. So all the information goes into the phone book, which 'remembers' hundreds of thousands of numbers for us. All books are places where we store facts and ideas, a simple example of 'information technology'.

A few people can do sums like '3678 times 2659' in their heads, but most of us would use a calculator to help. A large computer can do a 1000 million calculations like this every second.

Computers don't only do calculations. They are 'information processors' and can do many different jobs. That's why they are so useful. In many cities, computers control the traffic lights to reduce traffic jams. In offices, they help with writing letters. In factories computers control robots and other machines, and in banks they keep track of everyone's money.

This section of the book is mainly about computers and some of the things they can do – *information technology*.

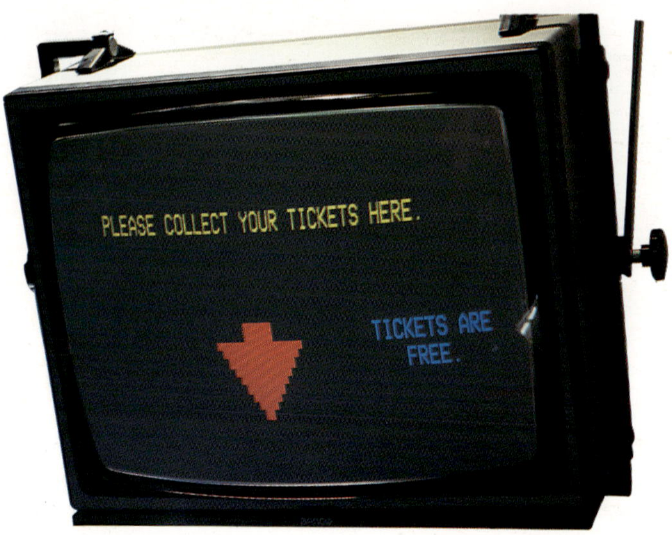

With the help of a small computer, a television screen turns into a noticeboard. This one provides information for people who come to LAUNCH PAD. It stores many different messages, and new ones can easily be added.

COMPUTER BOOKING SYSTEM

This computer booking system, used to arrange school visits to LAUNCH PAD, is an example of how a computer can help with office work. It writes thousands of letters to teachers every year.

All the information about the bookings is stored on one spinning disc which is coated with the same magnetic material as is used on video tapes.

HEAVY PEN

Computers are often used to control machinery. This is no easy job, particularly when the machinery is very heavy; it is hard to start and stop, and tends to 'overshoot'. You can feel the problem for yourself at the HEAVY PEN exhibit.

LOCK AND KEY

A key is like a message in code. The lock can 'read' the shape of the key. If the shape is right, then it is the correct key, and the lock will open. You can find out how the lock reads the shape of the key at the LOCK AND KEY exhibit.

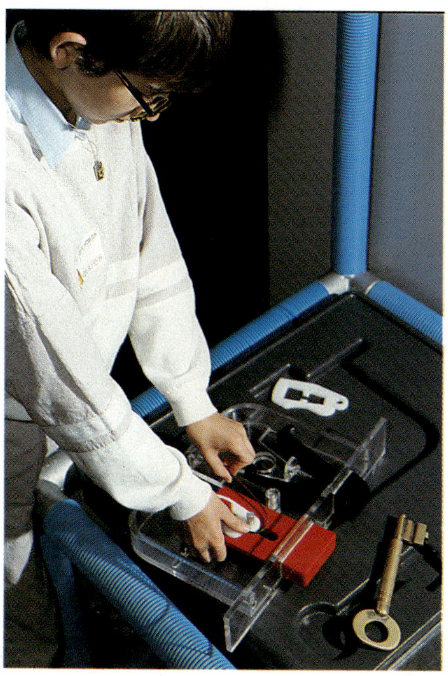

MUSEUM LINK – Punched cards

Machines which can be 'programmed' – given a sequence of instructions – have been made for many years. Often the program was in the form of cards or strips of paper with holes punched in them.

You can see some of these programmable machines in the *Textiles* and *Printing* galleries, and of course in the *Computing* gallery.

LAUNCH PAD Quiz – The first computer

'The first computer was designed before 1850.' True or false?

(Answer on page 49)

COMPUTER VIDEO

Computers do many different jobs, but in some ways all computers are the same: they all have some method of taking in information, such as a keyboard, and they all produce some sort of output, such as a picture on a screen. In between, they process the information in some way, using a 'program' to tell them what to do.

In the COMPUTER VIDEO exhibit the picture from a television camera is fed into a computer, which can change the picture in many different ways before sending it to the screen.

But before the computer can change the TV picture, it has to convert the picture into a series of numbers – because numbers are the only thing this sort of computer can work with.

So the picture from the TV camera is divided into 65 536 small rectangles, called pixels. Each of these is given a number to say exactly what brightness and colour it is.

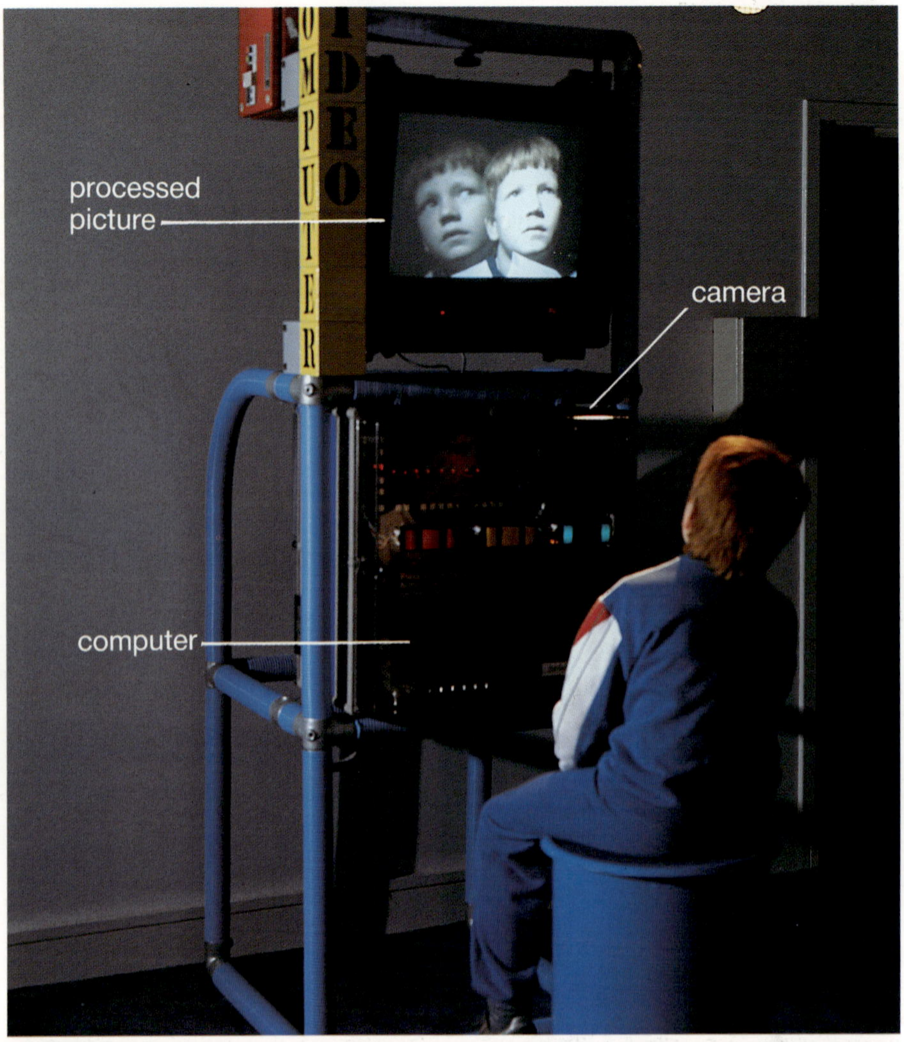

LAUNCH PAD Quiz – Pixel picture 1

This picture is made up of only 900 pixels. It shows a well-known person on children's television.

Can you see who it is?

(Answer on page 49)

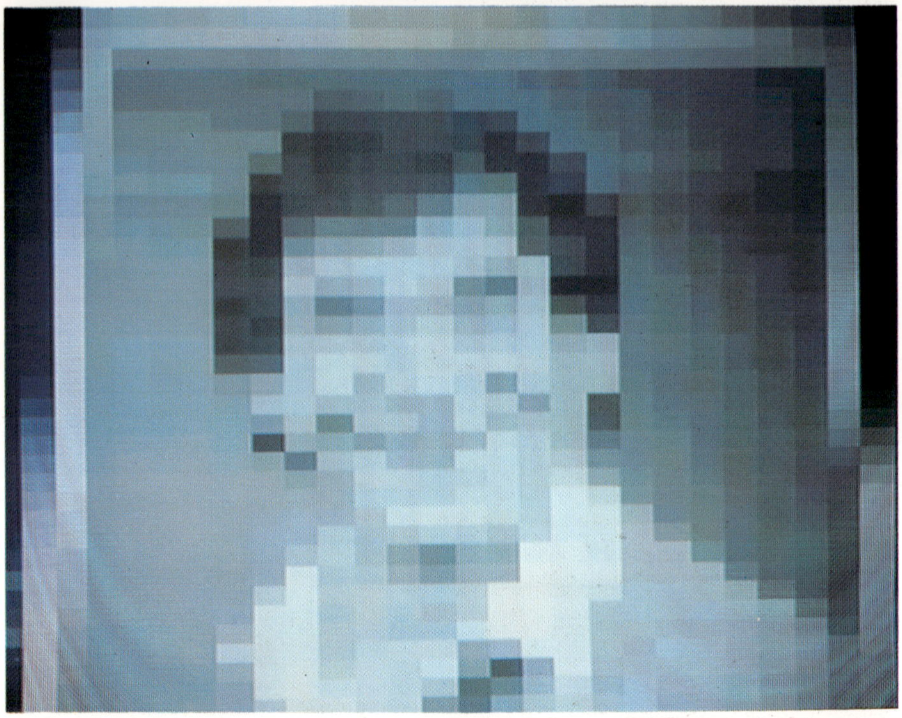

All these numbers go into the computer's memory and, according to what buttons have been pressed, they are changed in some way before being turned back into the picture you see on the screen.

For example, the computer might scan through all of the 65 536 numbers, pick out the ones that represent red pixels, and change them into the number that represents green pixels. We would then see a *false colour* picture on the screen.

Producing false colour is just one example of *image processing*, which is often used in making pop videos and other television programmes.

Scientists use image processing to bring out important details in pictures, and to help us see things which are normally invisible – as in the HEAT CAMERA exhibit.

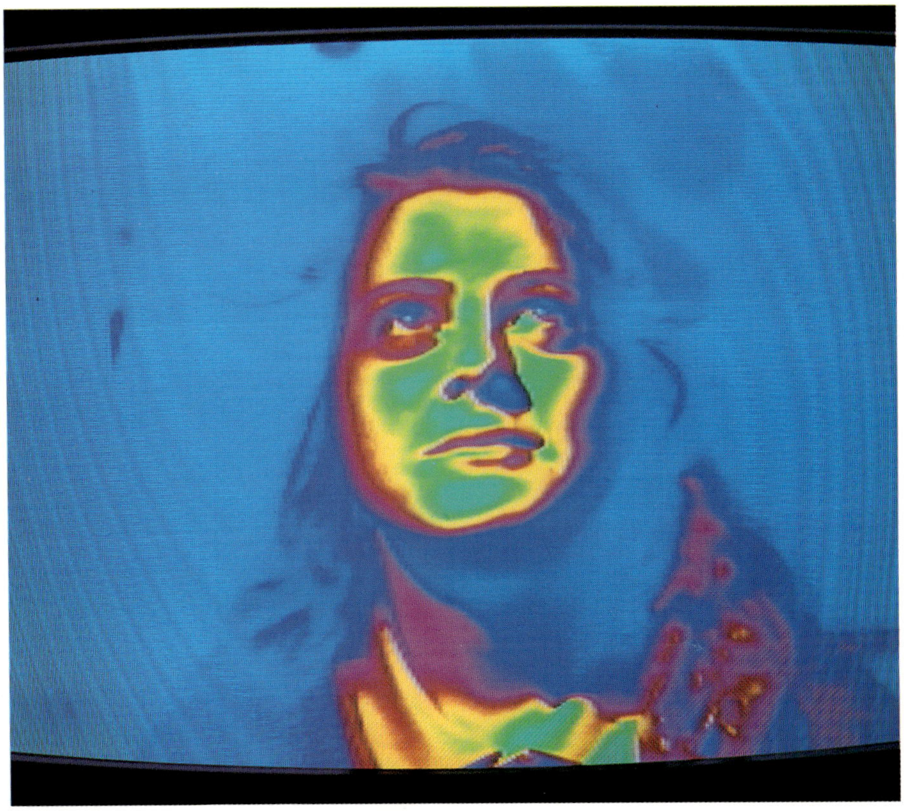

DAILY TELEGRAPH SPACE FRONTIERS

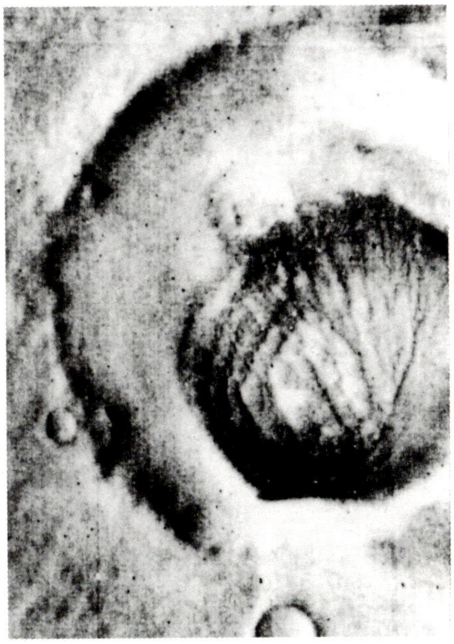

A crater on Mars recorded by the spacecraft Mariner 9. Left: the image as it was received on Earth.

Right: the same image after computer processing to bring out the details.

LAUNCH PAD at large – Computer TV

Look out for TV programmes and videos where computer image processing has been used – perhaps to change the colours or to break up the picture or make it flip over and fly about the screen.

LAUNCH PAD Quiz – Pixel picture 2

Here is a pattern made out of 24 small squares – *pixels*.

What does it turn into if you 'process' it by moving each pixel along one place?

To find out, use the second grid.

Copy number 1 in the top pattern into space 2 in the lower one, 2 into 3 and so on, ending by putting number 24 into space 1 of the lower grid.

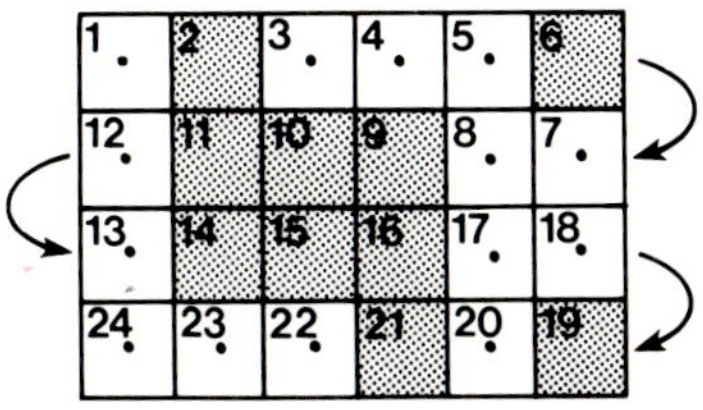

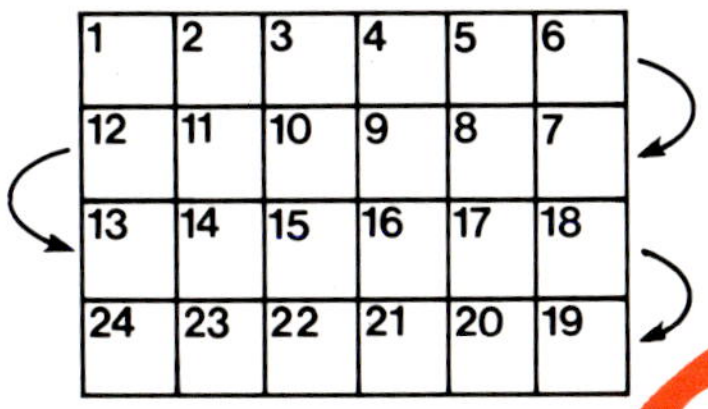

(Answer on page 49)

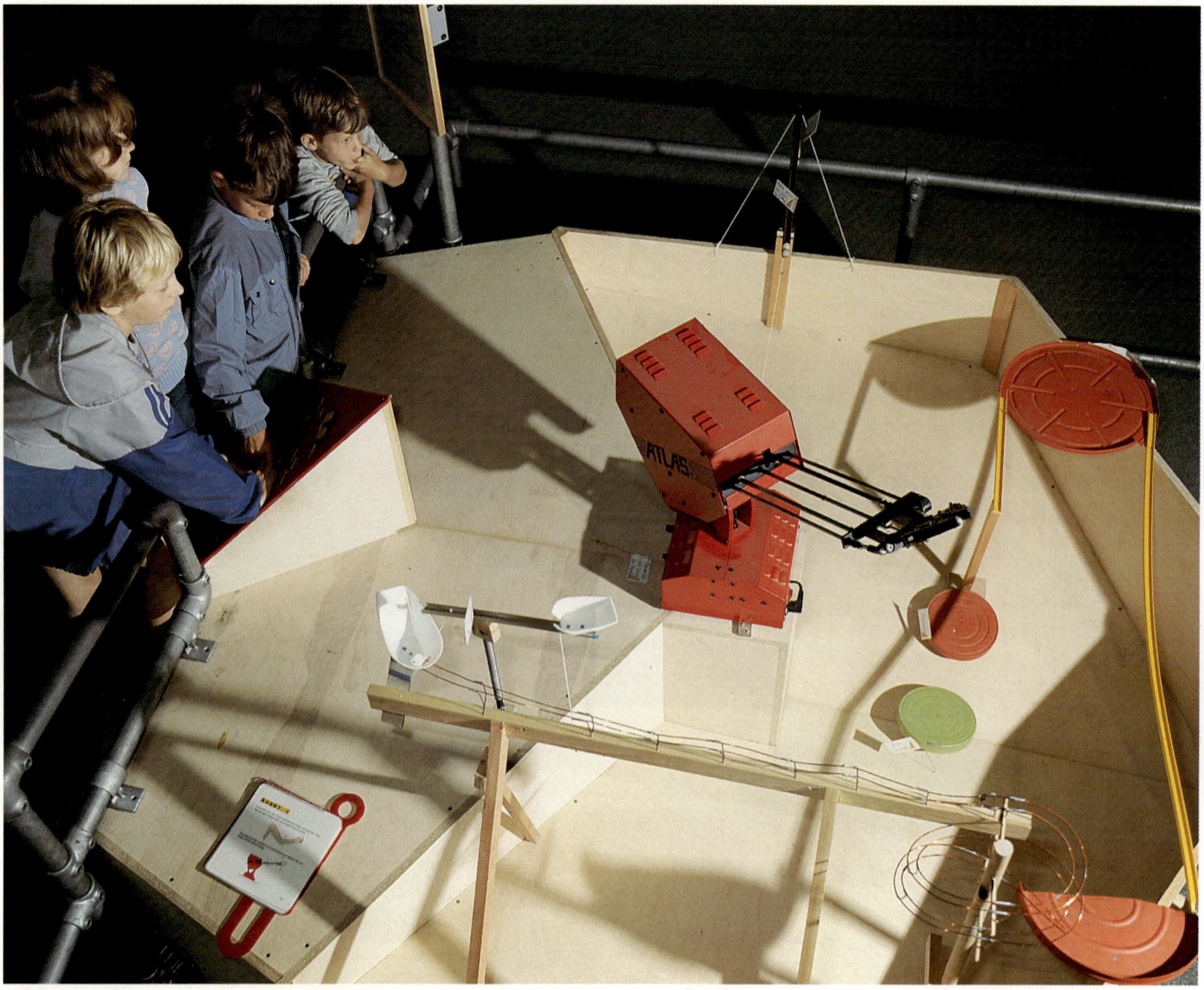

ROBOT

Our arms move and bend in many directions, and we can grip things with our fingers and thumbs. The mechanical arm in the ROBOT exhibit can do many of the same things.

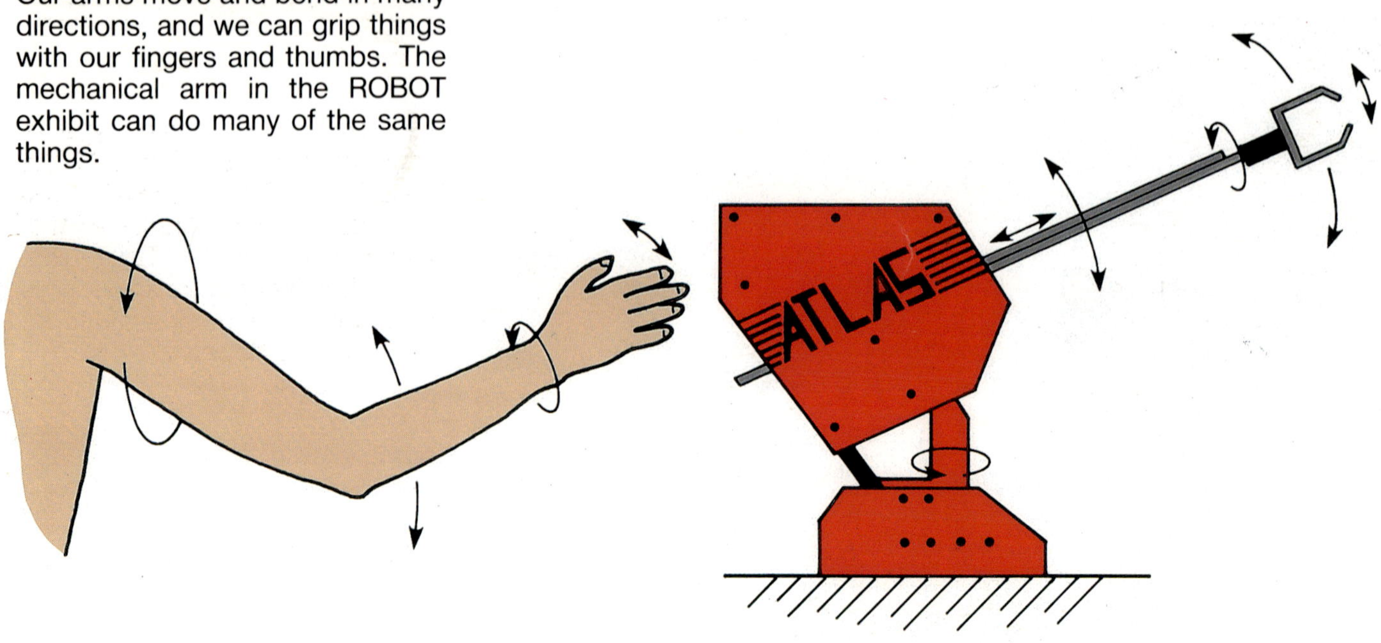

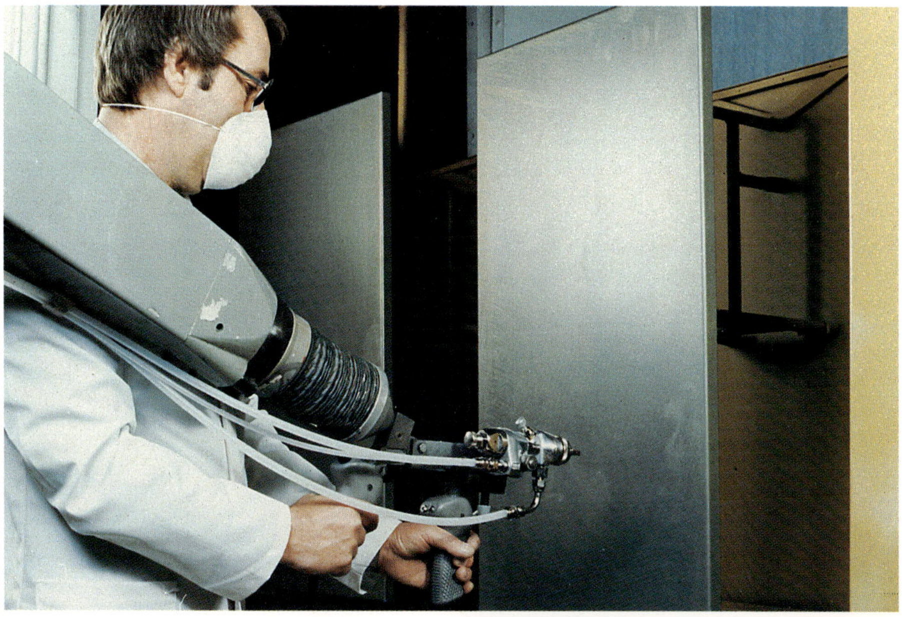

Each moving part of the robot is driven by a special electric motor, called a *stepper motor*. Ordinary motors turn steadily when supplied with electricity. A stepper motor only turns in small steps, all of equal size, and must be supplied with electricity in short bursts, or *pulses*.

When you move a switch, a computer sends electrical pulses to one of the stepper motors, so you can give the robot instructions to move the way you want. The computer also has a memory, so the robot can be made to repeat the same, simple movements over and over again.

The man is teaching a robot to use a paint spray: he does the job while the robot 'holds his hand' and learns exactly what movements to make. The robot can then repeat the movements by itself.

FORD MOTOR COMPANY

In Britain, robots were first used in 1980. They do jobs like painting and spot welding (joining pieces of metal together) in car factories.

TEACH THE TURTLE

The Turtle is a different type of robot, used for teaching. At the TEACH THE TURTLE exhibit you can write a short program – a list of instructions telling the Turtle what to do. The program is stored in a computer, which gives the instructions to the Turtle one at a time.

Technology to help our senses

Finding out

There are invisible things going on all around you – right now, as you read these words.

There are radio and TV waves streaming past, for example, but without a radio or TV set you cannot tell they are there. There is dust in the air around you, but the grains are too small to see. You yourself are giving out an invisible glow of heat, called *infra-red* (and so is everyone else), but our eyes cannot detect it.

We are born with a good set of senses – sight, touch, hearing and so on – and they seem to give us a good picture of everything around us. But much of the world is in fact quite hidden from us. Our senses need help to discover it. We can use a microscope, for example: the most powerful microscopes would make a pea look the size of a mountain.

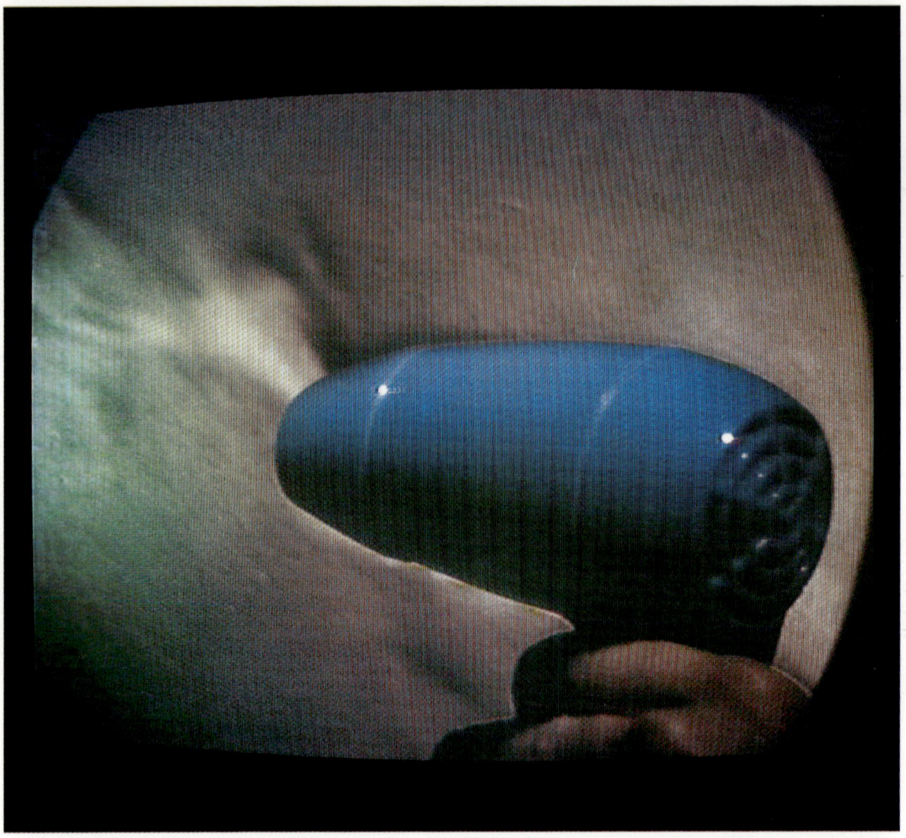

LAUNCH PAD is full of air, but the only place where we can see it is in the VISIBLE AIR exhibit. A special TV system lets us see currents of air flowing past things that are warm.

We have even given ourselves completely new senses. We use X-rays and neutron beams to 'see' through things, and our radio telescopes can pick up 'whispers' of radio waves many millions of light-years away in space.

There are exhibits in LAUNCH PAD which show how we can make our senses more useful, and exhibits which show what it is like to have a completely new sense. This section tells you about some of them.

SHAKE HANDS

The black plastic bowl is shiny enough to act like a mirror. It is curved and so creates an unusual kind of mirror image – one you can shake hands with. The image of your hand is called a *real* image – rays of light really do form the image, in about the same place as your hand.

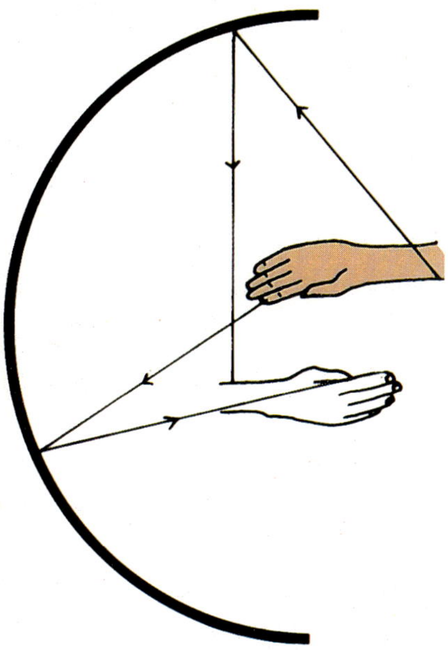

But in an ordinary flat mirror, the image appears **behind** the mirror. This is not a real image because no light rays can actually pass through the mirror. The image is created as much by your eyes as by the mirror.

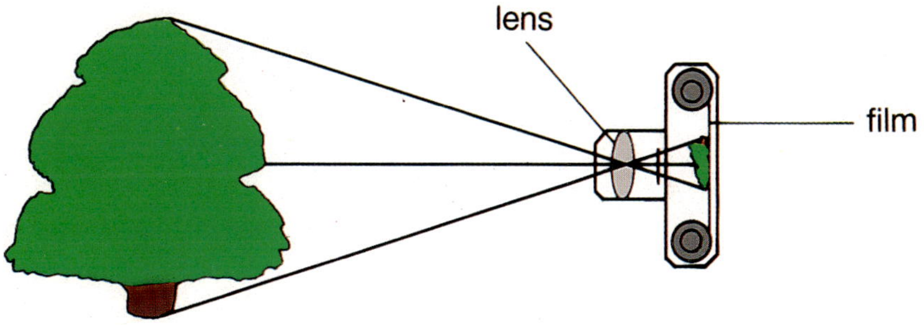

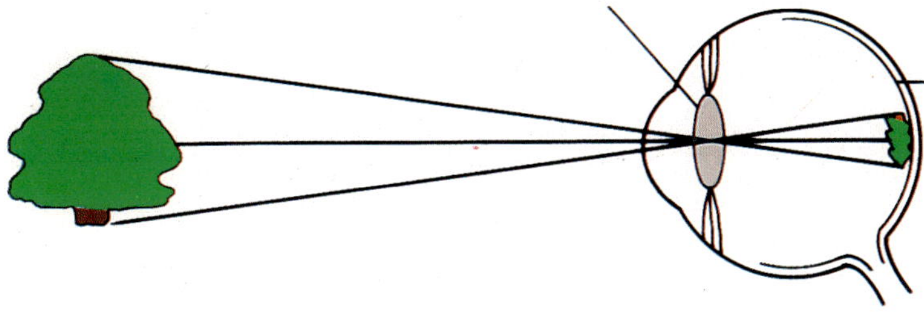

Real images can also be created by lenses.

The lens system of a camera captures real images on photographic film. Focusing the camera on a near or distant object adjusts the position of the image so that it always falls sharply on the film. The lens system of the eye places a real image on the retina.

CALIFORNIA INSTITUTE OF TECHNOLOGY

Many large telescopes use a curved mirror to produce real images of distant stars. The mirror acts as a 'light collector' to make bright images of very faint stars. The image is then magnified by a lens – like viewing it through a magnifying glass.

The largest mirror at the Mount Palomar Observatory, California, shown without its reflective coating, whilst being cleaned.

LAUNCH PAD Quiz – Giant mirror

The world's largest telescope mirror is

about three metres across?
about six metres across?
about nine metres across?

(Answer on page 49)

MUSEUM LINK – Telescope mirrors

You can find some large curved mirrors, used in telescopes, in the *Astronomy* gallery. The biggest one weighs nearly four tonnes.

HEAT CAMERA

Everything around you gives out *infra-red radiation.* Warm things, like your face and hands, give out more radiation than cool ones.

Your eyes cannot detect infra-red radiation, but the HEAT CAMERA can. On the screen, warm things are shown in red or yellow, and cooler ones look blue or black (see photograph on page 1).

TIPTOE TESTER

The TIPTOE TESTER detects the vibrations made by someone walking along the platform. You can see the detector in the picture, under the dome at the far end.

A vibration makes the coil of wire in the detector move in and out of the detector's magnet. This movement generates a small electric current in the coil (in a similar way to the generators in the PEDAL POWER exhibit). The current is amplified (increased) and used to switch the lights on the end panel.

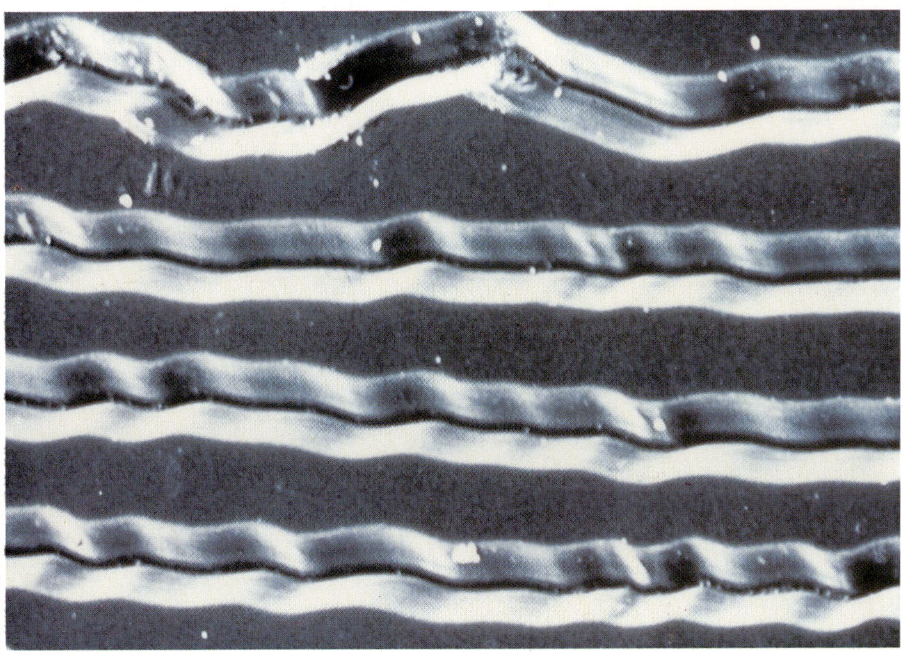

DR TONY BRAIN/SCIENCE PHOTO LIBRARY

Record players are also vibration detectors. The vibration of the needle in the record groove creates a varying electric current: this is amplified by the amplifier and turned into sound by the speakers.

The strength of the current and the way it varies determine the loudness, pitch and quality of the final sound.

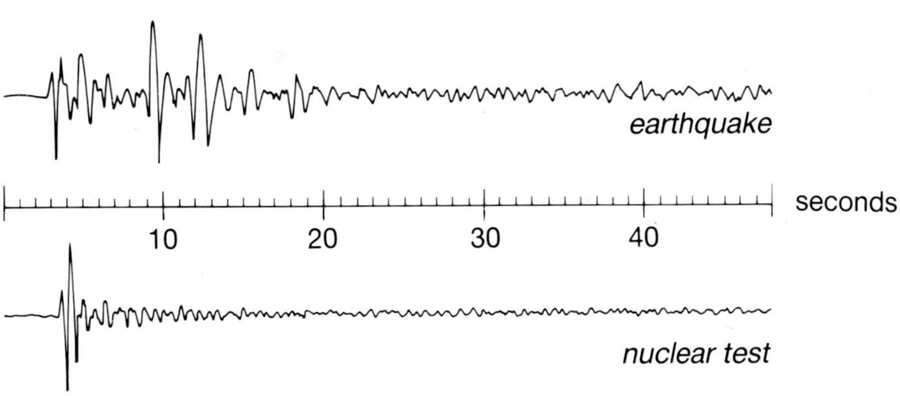

Very sensitive vibration detectors – seismographs – are used to detect and record earthquakes. They can also be used to detect underground nuclear bomb test explosions. Normally a nuclear bomb test produces a much simpler seismograph trace than an earthquake of the same strength.

The earthquake and the nuclear bomb test both took place in the USSR, about 7500 km away from the detector in Canada.

WATCHDOG

The WATCHDOG exhibit uses the *Doppler effect* to detect moving things. It is the Doppler effect that makes a fire engine's siren sound higher when it is approaching you than when it has passed. This happens because sound is a stream of waves. When the fire engine approaches you, the sound waves 'catch up' with one another and become crowded together so that the frequency (pitch) of the sound is increased.

Instead of sound waves, the WATCHDOG sends out ultrasound – sound which is too high-pitched to hear. When the ultrasound wave bounces off something moving towards it, the 'echo' or reflected wave is compressed so its frequency is increased.

By comparing this echo with the original ultrasound, the Watchdog can tell whether something is moving near it. The 'growl' it makes has a frequency equal to the difference between the emitted sound and its echo, so the faster you move, the higher is the sound.

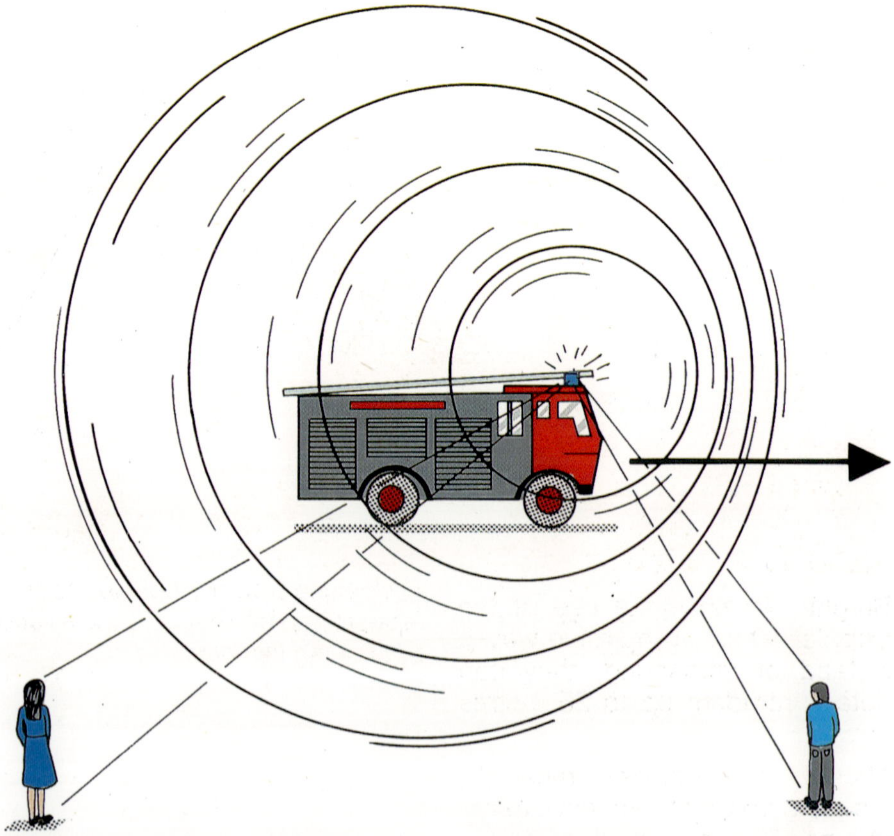

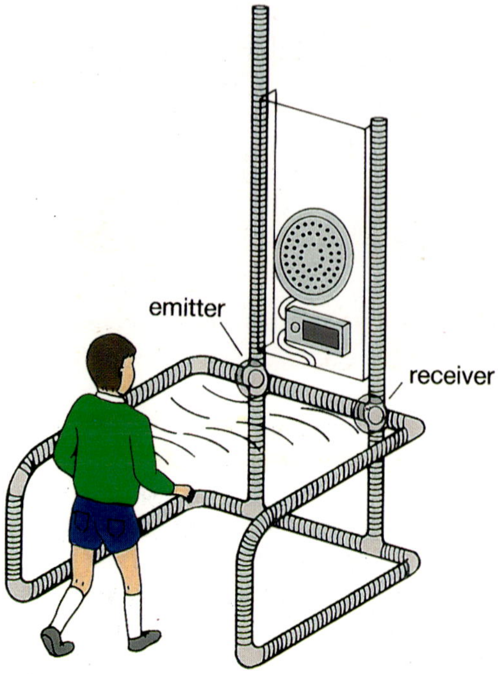

DALE PRODUCTS

Police use Doppler devices as a 'speed trap' to measure the speed of passing vehicles.

MULLARD LTD

Some traffic lights are fitted with Doppler radar devices so that they can detect approaching vehicles and turn red or green as appropriate.

Burglar alarms make use of the Doppler effect. Using radio waves instead of ultrasound, they can detect intruders up to 25 metres away.

Aircraft use Doppler radar to measure their speed relative to the ground. The effect is also used in military equipment to detect moving objects automatically and at a distance.

The Horseshoe bat uses ultrasound to detect movement – like the beating of an insect's wings.

STEPHEN DALTON/NHPA

LAUNCH PAD at home – TV colours

Use a magnifying glass to look closely at the screen of a colour TV set. (A clear marble held close to the screen also works well.)

Can you see that the whole picture, and all the different colours, are built up from very small bars which are either red, green or blue?

How do these bars change when the colours in the picture change?

COLOUR BOX

In the COLOUR BOX exhibit you can see how your clothes look in different coloured lights. You can also see what happens when you mix the three primary lights – red, green and blue – in different ways. All the colours in this picture were made by mixing red, green and blue.

BIG OPTICS

The giant lens in the BIG OPTICS exhibit can be used as a magnifying glass. Unlike a normal lens which is curved, it is made from a flat sheet of plastic. This has tiny steps in it to bend the light as it comes through.

This sort of lens is used in car headlights to make the beam of light spread in the right direction.

LOOK HERE

The light from an ordinary electric lamp – or from the sun – is really a mixture of colours, but our eyes cannot see them. With the help of a *diffraction grating,* part of the LOOK HERE exhibit, the hidden colours in LAUNCH PAD are revealed.

MUSEUM LINK – Earthquakes

There is more about earthquakes, and the way they are detected, in the *Geophysics* gallery on the third floor.

Technology to help our senses

Communi-cating

The Battle of Trafalgar was fought on a Monday. Nobody in England knew what the result was until the following Wednesday fortnight – 16 days later. Communications were slow in 1805!

Today we don't have to wait that long for the news. With television we can watch events on the other side of the world, as they happen. And by telephone we can be connected from our homes to any one of the 600 million other telephones in the world.

Communication is essential to each one of us, and vital to the sort of society we live in. Every time we speak we use a complicated system of coded sounds – words – to send information and ideas to someone else.

When writing was invented, about 3500 years BC, civilisation was able to make progress because each generation could build on the ideas and discoveries of previous generations. The knowledge of the Ancient Greeks was forgotten for centuries during the Dark Ages, but because it was written down, it was later rediscovered and led to the beginnings of modern science.

The invention of the electric telegraph in 1837 was the start of really fast communications. It was soon followed by the telephone and the 'mass media' such as newspapers, radio and TV, which have become so important in providing what we know – and think – about the world.

This section is about the exhibits in LAUNCH PAD which help you discover how some of these new ways of communicating work – *communications technology.*

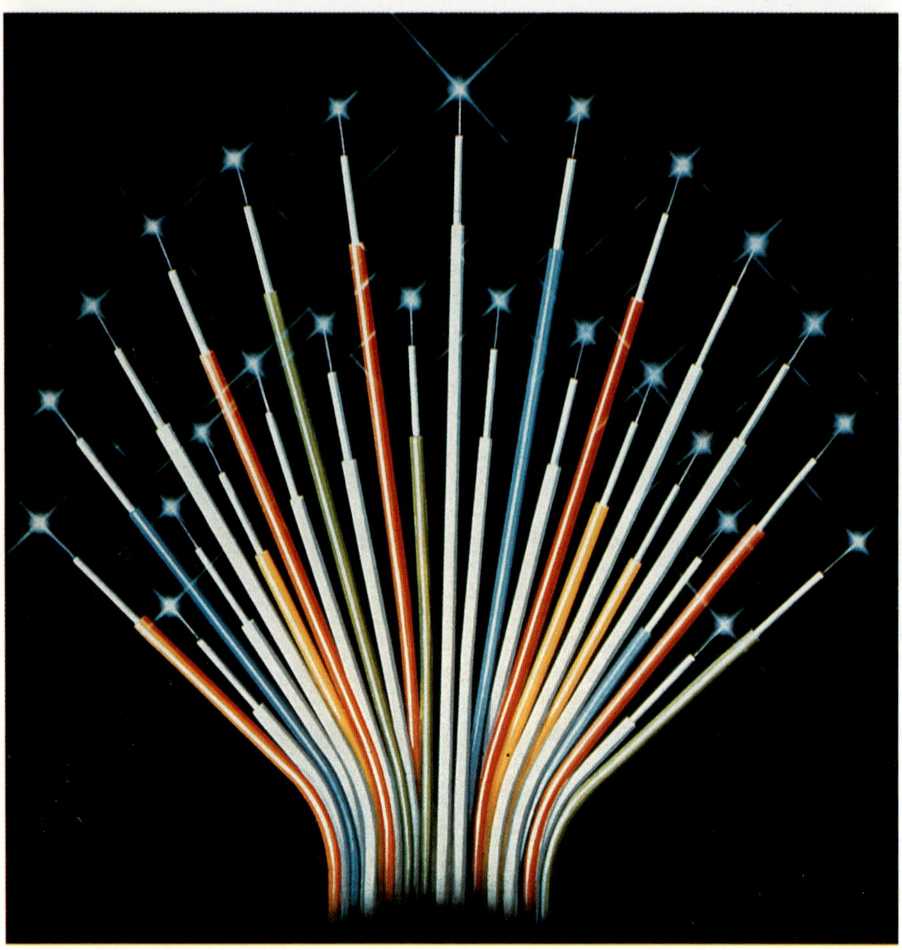

BRITISH TELECOM

LIGHT PIPES

In space, light travels in straight lines – but it will also follow the curve of a strand of transparent material. This is the principle of *fibre optics* and of the perspex tubes in the LIGHT PIPES exhibit.

If you looked through the end of a fish-tank, you would be able to see through the water and out of the opposite end of the tank. But if you look towards the sides, you see only a reflection – at this shallow angle, light is reflected from the boundary between the glass fish-tank and air.

Light is piped along an optical fibre in the same way. It is reflected at the boundary between the two glasses that make up the fibre, and only emerges at the end.

Technology to help our senses

Optical fibres are used to carry information along many telephone lines. A light message can travel up to 50 km at a stretch without 'boosting'. The map shows which links in Britain's telephone network will be made with optical fibres by 1988.

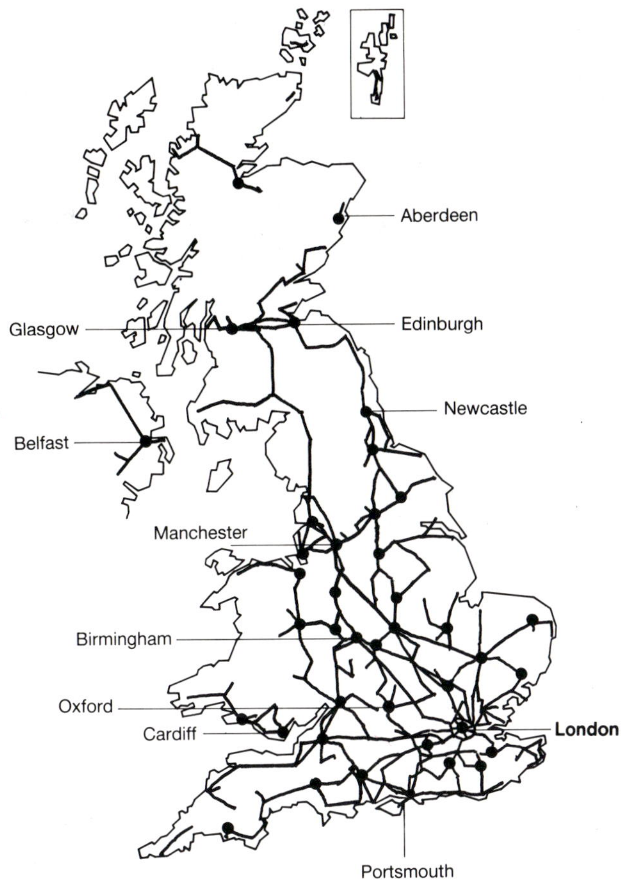

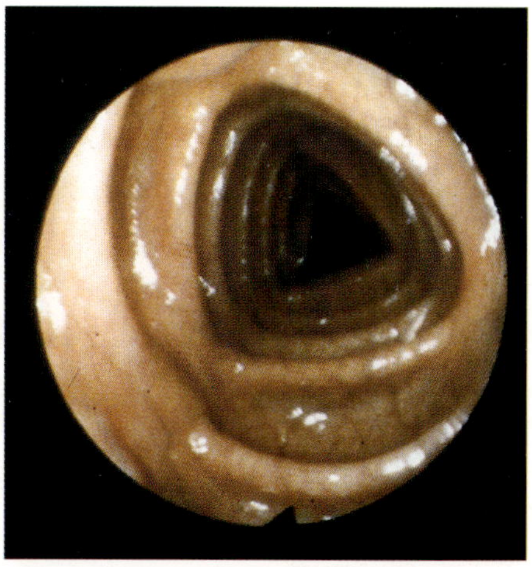

Optical fibres are also used to examine parts of the body which would otherwise be inaccessible – like the large intestine.

MUSEUM LINK – Fibre optics

You can find out about fibre optics and their uses in the *Telecommunications* gallery (cases L18–L25), in the *Optics* gallery (case F27) and in *The Science and Art of Medicine* gallery on the fifth floor of the Museum (cases T41–T45).

LAUNCH PAD Quiz – Watching the box

If all the TV programmes seen by an average person in Britain in one year were put end to end, how long would they last?

less than one week?
between one week and one month?
more than one month?

(Answer on page 49)

LAUNCH PAD Quiz – Using the phone

On average, how many phone calls does every person in Britain make in one year?

About 25
About 100
About 400

(Answer on page 49)

TV AERIAL

The aerial in this exhibit is a Yagi aerial, invented in 1928 by the Japanese scientist, Hidetsugu Yagi.

Television is transmitted as electromagnetic waves which travel at the speed of light (about 1 100 000 000km per hour). The aerial absorbs some of the energy of these waves and converts it – and the information it carries – into electricity.

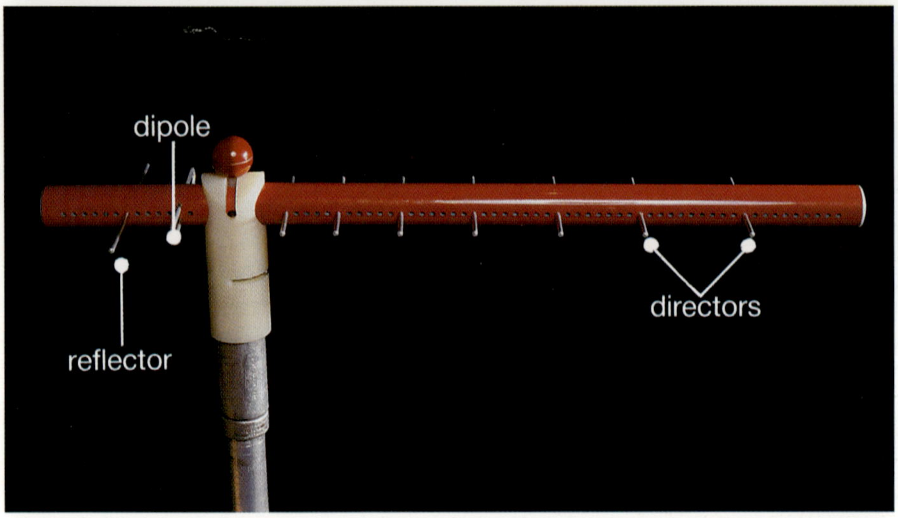

The reflector is the largest piece of metal. It reflects the waves back towards the dipole. The smaller rods, the directors, 'focus' the waves towards the dipole. The dipole converts the waves and their information to electricity which then reaches the TV set through a wire.

The Yagi aerial picks up only those waves which travel along the direction in which the aerial points. So it avoids interference from waves reflected by hills or other objects.

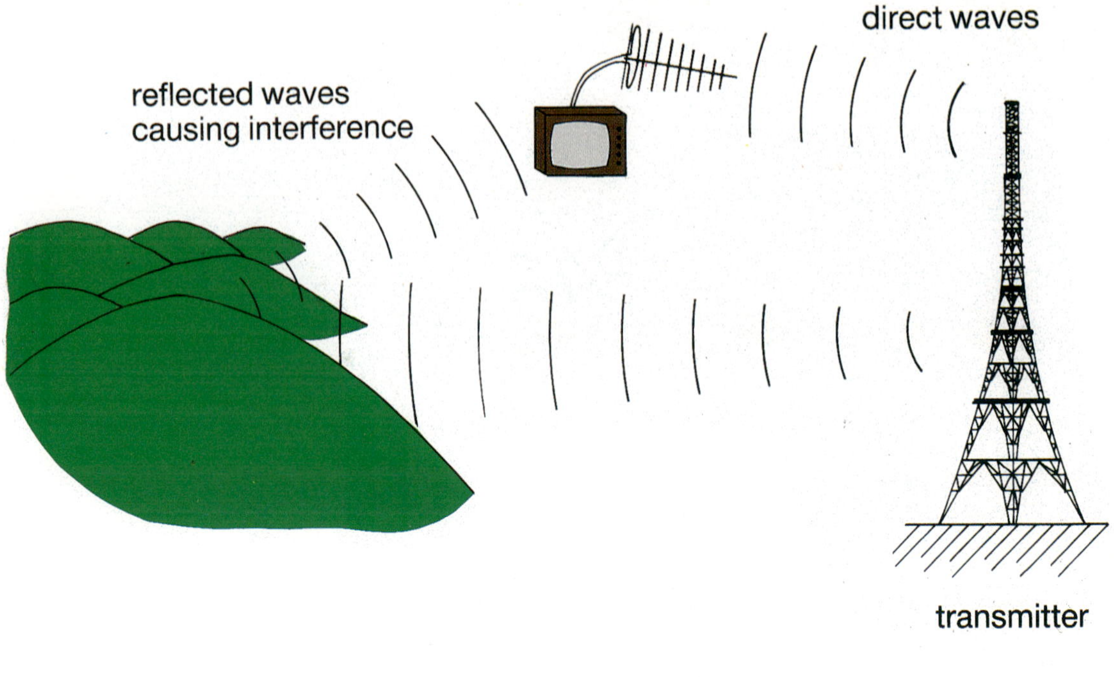

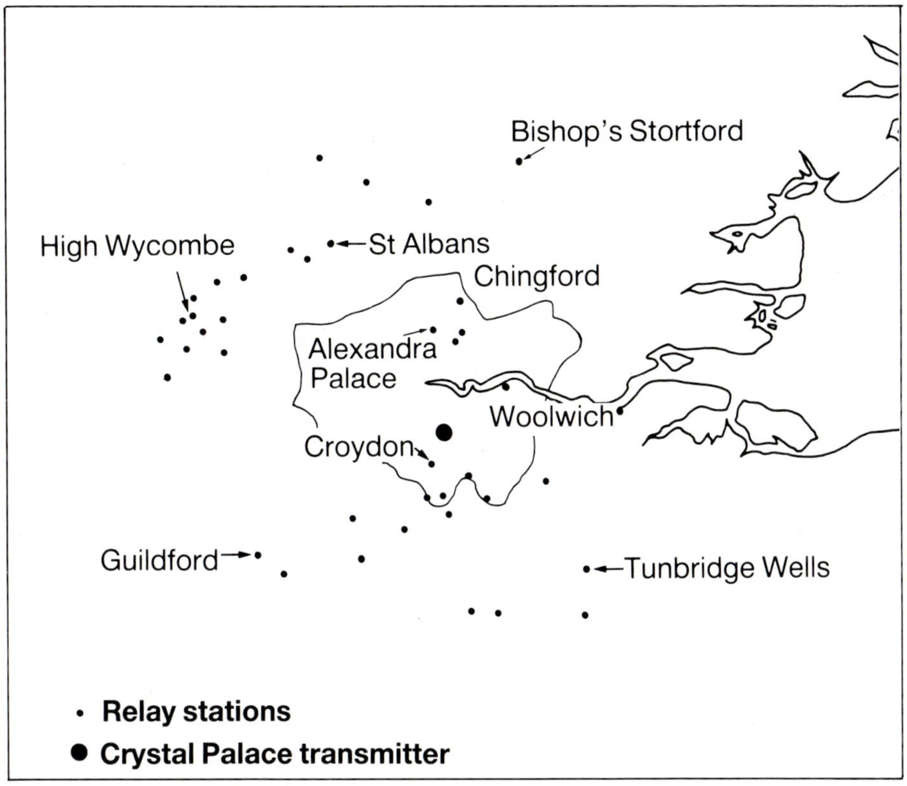

The map shows the position of TV transmitters and relay stations in the London area. The relay stations receive the transmission from the main station (Crystal Palace) and retransmit it at a different frequency. Local TV sets tune to this different frequency to avoid interference from the main transmission.

The transmitter for this exhibit is actually inside the Museum. Like the relay stations, it converts the BBC transmission to a different frequency and the exhibit TV set is tuned to this.

TV AND MAGNET

The picture on a TV screen is made by electrons which hit the inside of the screen. If you hold a magnet near the screen, it pushes these electrons, so that they hit the wrong places on the screen and make the wrong colours. *(Do not try this on your TV at home. You may damage it.)*

BEAMED VOICES

The BEAMED VOICES exhibit uses **no** special equipment and your voice is **not** amplified: the effect is caused by the precise shape of the dishes which reflect and concentrate your voice so that it can be 'beamed' across a crowded room and heard on the other side.

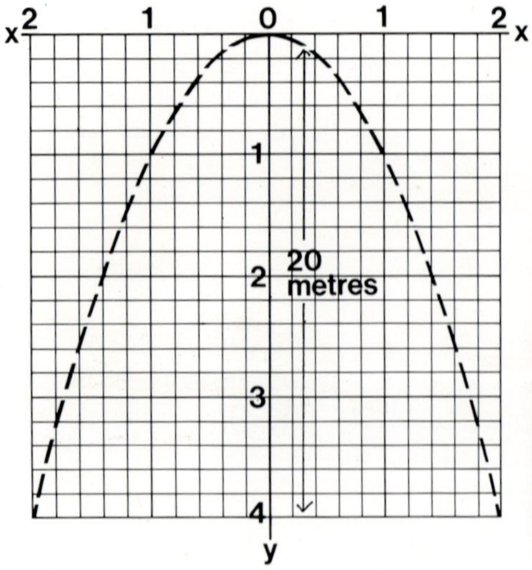

The curve of the dishes is part of a shape called a parabola. A bouncing ball, or a ball you throw, also traces out a parabola.

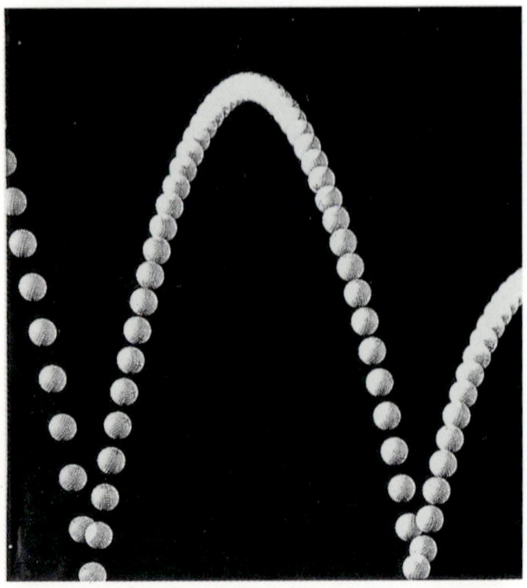

H. EDGERTON

A parabola reflects soundwaves – or any other waves – in a special way.

If you stand at the right point (the focus) and speak towards the dish, your voice is reflected from the dish to form a straight parallel beam: this travels to the other dish where it is reflected to a point again. Because the beam is parallel, very little sound is lost on the way.

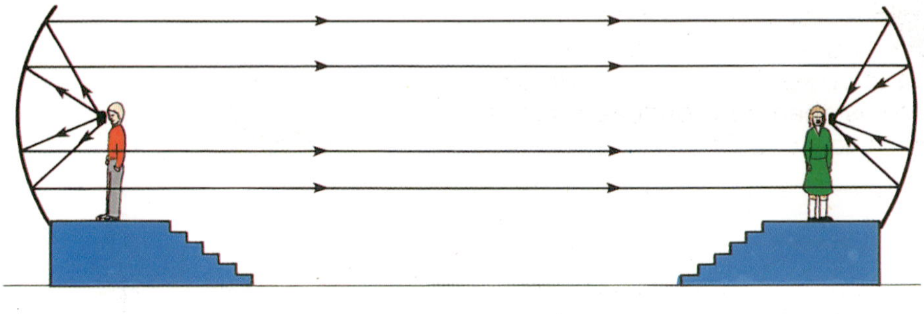

Technology to help our senses

Radiotelescopes use parabolic dish reflectors to collect radio waves emitted by distant stars and galaxies.

This radiotelescope (sited near Bonn in West Germany) has a dish 100 m in diameter – the largest radiotelescope dish in the world.

If you telephone someone in the USA from Britain, the message is often transmitted as radio waves instead of travelling along a wire.

It cannot be beamed straight between the two countries, because of the curvature of the earth. So it is beamed up to a communications satellite, using a parabolic dish, and then beamed back down to earth.

Consequently, the message travels about 72 000 km, and takes about a quarter of a second. (This causes a half-second time delay between speaking and hearing a reply, which makes conversation quite strange.)

Intelsat satellites are used for long-distance telephone lines and international TV transmissions.

At present there are 12 Intelsat satellites, each stationed above a different part of the world. Normally the TV transmission (or telephone message) is received from the satellite by one of two large parabolic dish receivers in Britain, and is then re-broadcast across the whole country.

However, small parabolic dishes are now available which can be installed outside individual houses to receive the broadcast directly from the satellite. They act like a very efficient aerial to 'concentrate' the TV transmission. Since 1982 several independent satellite TV channels have been set up to broadcast in this way.

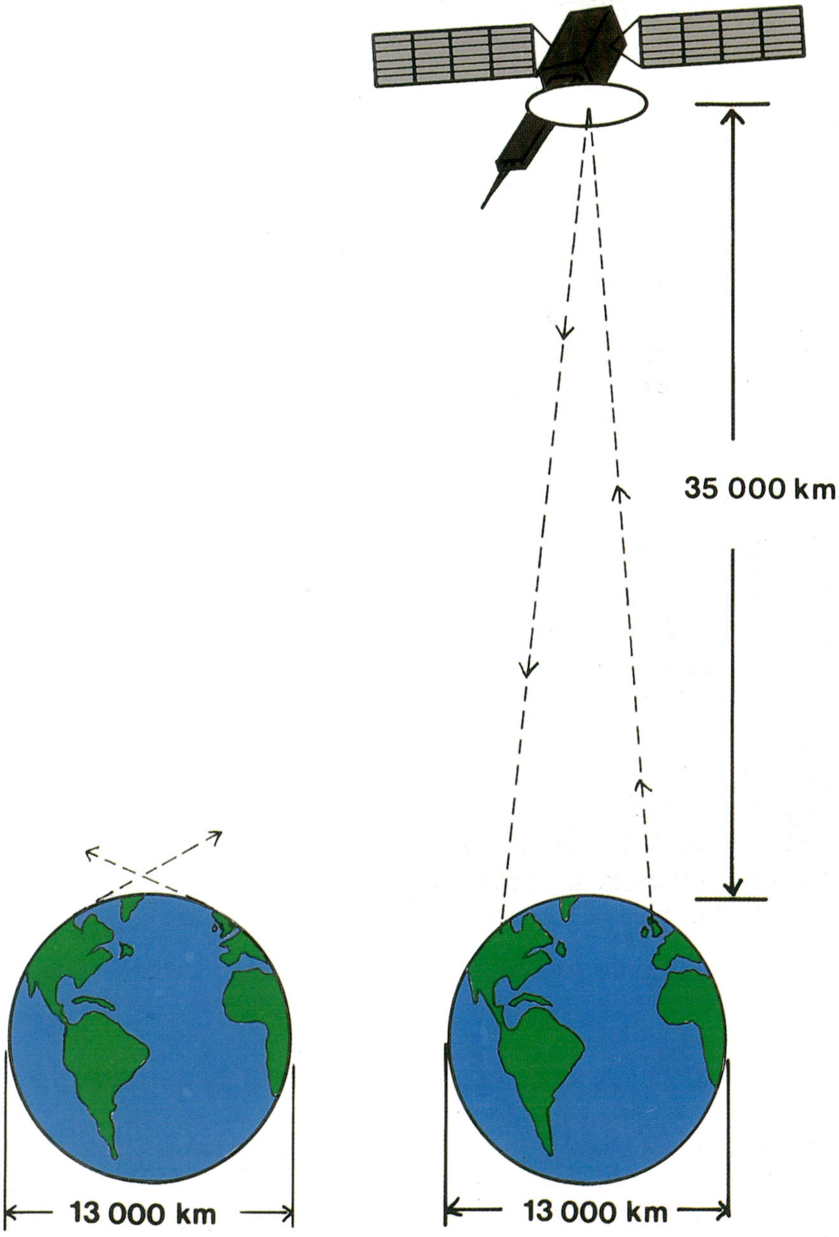

FLASHWORDS

At the FLASHWORDS exhibit, ghostly words appear in space. A strip of seven lights flashes the word, bit by bit, very quickly. When you move your eyes past the strip, you see the whole word at once. This is because of *persistence of vision* – the way your eyes still 'see' something for a moment after it has really gone.

TV and films work in the same way. Separate pictures flash onto the screen very quickly, but you just see a steady picture.

LAUNCH PAD at home – Flashing pictures

Here's a simple experiment which shows you something about how television works:

Switch on the television set, and then draw the curtains and switch off the lights in the room.

Hold up a white ruler, or a rolled-up newspaper, so that it is lit up by the light from the TV screen.

Watch the ruler or newspaper while you wave it up and down quickly. What do you see?

Can you work out how this shows that the TV screen is really flashing on and off many times each second?

LAUNCH PAD at large – Big dishes

Look out for dish aerials, used for sending and receiving radio and television waves. Why are they usually on the tops of buildings?

Can you tell whether the dish is for communicating with a satellite or with another dish on the Earth's surface?

Look out for other parabolic reflectors too – in torches and car headlamps for example.

LAUNCH PAD Quiz – Moving pictures

Every television programme is made up of many *still* pictures flashed onto the screen one after another.

How many separate pictures make up a half-hour programme

about 900?
about 90 000?
about 90 000 000?

(Answer on page 49)

LAUNCH PAD at home – PUZZLE PAGE

You can make your own version of some of the LAUNCH PAD puzzles, and try them on your friends.

To do these puzzles you have to think about the shapes of things, and the way different parts fit together.

Engineers and designers often have to be good at this sort of thinking.

Pentominoes

A pentomino is a shape made from five squares joined together.

Make a large copy of each of these five pentominoes, and cut them out from card:

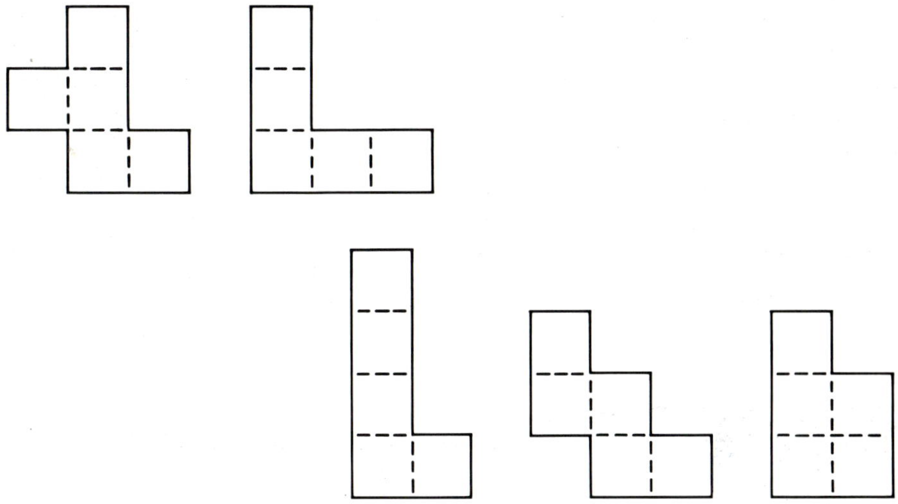

Can you fit them together, like a jig-saw puzzle, to make one large square?

If that was too easy, see how many other pentomino shapes you can make. There are 12 different ones altogether.

Can you fit all 12 pentominoes together to make a large rectangle?

Cubes

To make this puzzle you need 27 sugar lumps (they must be cubes) and some Blu-tak. Alternatively, you can use 27 children's building blocks, and plenty of sellotape.

Stick the cubes firmly together to make these seven pieces:

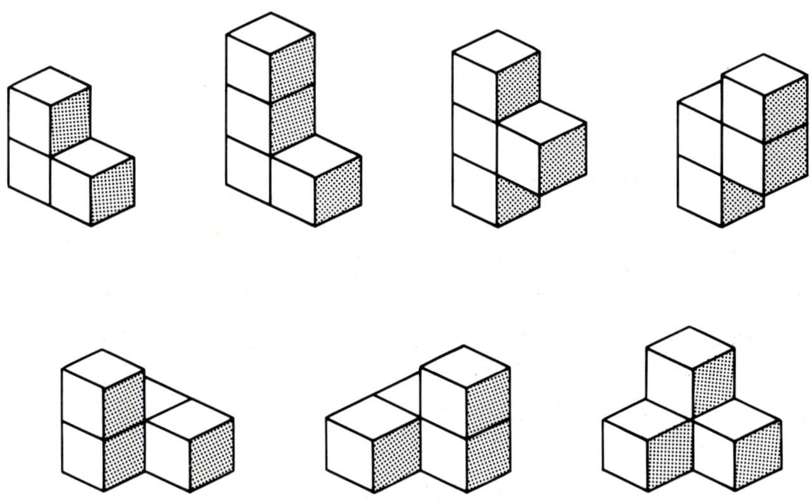

The puzzle is to fit all seven pieces together to form one large cube.

When you've done that, see what other simple shapes you can make out of these pieces.

Tetrahedron

A tetrahedron is a box with four sides:

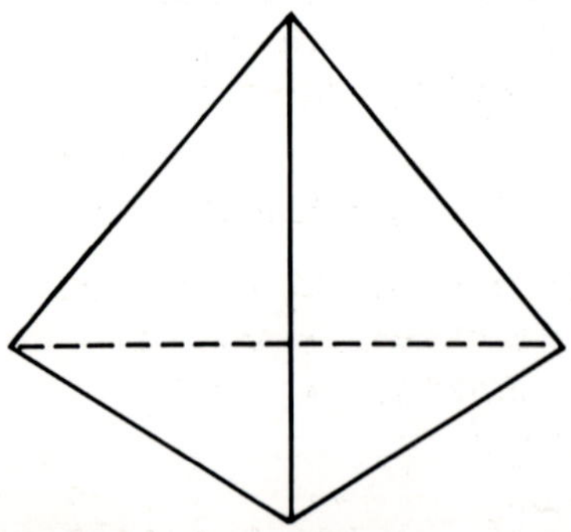

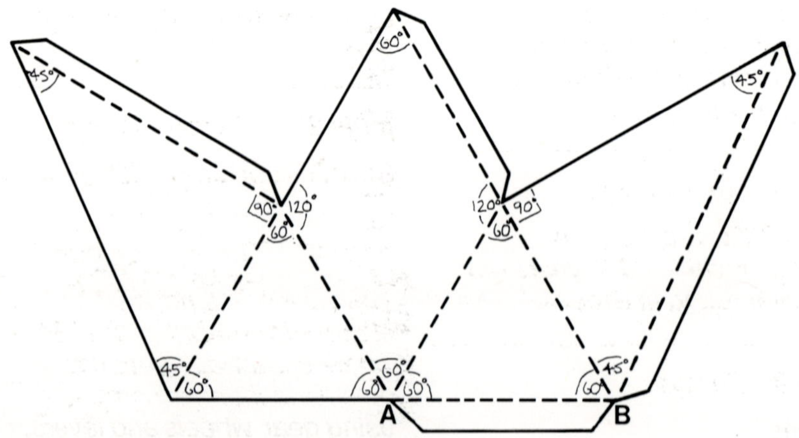

In this puzzle you have to make a tetrahedron by fitting together four smaller pieces. You will need a pencil, ruler, protractor, scissors and paste.

First make a larger copy of the shape on a piece of thick paper or thin card. Use a ruler and protractor. Start by making the line AB 5 centimetres long.

Cut out the shape, and draw round it to make three more copies. Cut them out too.

Score along the dotted lines, fold, and stick the flaps, to make four pieces like the one in the picture.

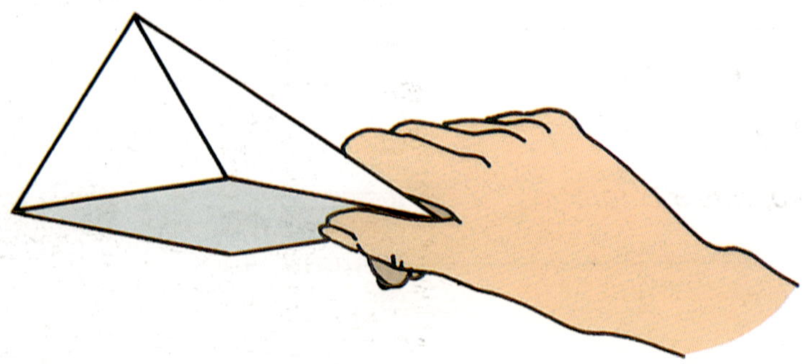

Can you find how to fit the pieces together to make a tetrahedron?

People have always had to find the answer to puzzles – the real-life problems like 'What is the best way to lift water from the bottom of a well?' and 'How can we make the roof of a house so that it won't leak?

And with real-life problems you can't look up the answers.

Thousands of years ago there was nobody to tell the first people how to grind corn. And today there's nobody to tell us how to send an expedition to Mars or how to stop people getting cancer. We have to work it out for ourselves.

We are not giving you the answers to the puzzles on these pages – so that you can feel what it is like to have to find your own solutions.

Have you found LAUNCH PAD and *The LAUNCH PAD Book* interesting? Do you enjoy solving puzzles and finding new ways to do things? If so, try to find out more about the people – engineers, scientists, technologists – whose life's work is discovering the answer to puzzles and inventing ways to do things which have never been done before.